Indiana University
Sinor Research Institute for Inner Asian Studies

PAPERS ON INNER ASIA

Devin DeWeese and Ron Sela, *Editors*

T0349910

NO. 42
(Subseries: Tibetan Studies)

Papers on Inner Asia

No. 42

Lucia Galli

Centre de recherche sur les civilisations de l'Asie orientale

TIBETAN "ILLICITNESS": FACETS OF ILLEGAL ECONOMY IN MID-2OTH-CENTURY KALIMPONG

INDIANA UNIVERSITY

SINOR RESEARCH INSTITUTE FOR INNER ASIAN STUDIES

Bloomington, Indiana

2021

Papers on Inner Asia is a refereed occasional paper series focused on the history, language, literature, and culture of Inner Asia. Inner Asia is defined as the region that includes Islamic Central Asia (the areas sometimes called Western, Eastern, and Afghan Turkestan), Mongolia, Manchuria, and Tibet. The papers deal with various topics related to this vast region, in fields of history, philology, linguistics, anthropology, archeology, and economics, among others. Works on certain subjects that transcend the boundaries of Inner Asia in its strict sense, but are relevant for the study of its peoples, languages, history, and culture, are also included.

The *Papers* were launched by Yuri Bregel in 1986. Beginning in 2020, the series is divided into six sub-series: (1) Islamic Central Asia; (2) Volga-Ural region and Western Siberia; (3) Mongolian and Manchu Studies; (4) Tibetan Studies; (5) Inner Asia through the Twelfth Century; and (6) The Mongol Empire, Thirteenth-Fourteenth Centuries.

Papers on Inner Asia is designed to ensure prompt publication of scholarly papers and to facilitate the publication of longer papers, which are large enough not to be accepted by most scholarly journals. For further inquiries see sinor.indiana.edu

ABSTRACT

Illegal economies and borderlands are intrinsically connected: geographical remoteness, weak state control, and dynamic social texture provide the kind of "grey" zone wherein a shadow economy may thrive. The present article aims to explore one of such middle grounds by focusing on the evolution of market-based crimes in Kalimpong between the mid-1930s and the early 1960s: the timeframe, deliberately limited to the years preceding WWII up to the Sino-Indian war of 1962, embraces the most active period in the history of the Himalayan trade hub. From remote hill station to main centre of the land route connecting Lhasa to Calcutta, Kalimpong was a hotbed of illicit activities – a vital node in several criminal distribution networks as well as a site of local production and consumption of illegal commodities. Availing myself of contemporary sources, such as local newspapers and official and legal documents drafted at government and district levels, I will decode the national and supranational conditions that triggered the emergence first, and the decline later, of Kalimpong as a trans-Himalayan "contact zone" and explore how these affected the lives of those Tibetans who operated across the line – of both state and legality.

Introduction

On January 20, 2021, Chinese and Indian troops reportedly engaged in a minor face-off at the Nathu La pass, in north Sikkim. The incident, presented by *Times of India* as a "brawl",[1] was the latest of a series of clashes and skirmishes that kept flaring up along the Sino-Indian border since June 15-16, 2020, when twenty Indian soldiers died in melee fighting along the Line of Actual Control (LAC). The following stand-off in the Ladakh sector and reciprocal accusations of encroachment ignited nationalist feelings in India, a political show-off that did little to dampen the trade between the two super-powers. On March 6, 2021, amidst cries for boycotts of Chinese products, the telecom equipment company Huawei bagged a multimillion-dollar network contract from Bharti Airtel,[2] and that despite global concerns of cyber-related threats from Chinese companies.

Two features of this story – growing economic interdependence and a persistent territorial dispute – are a recurring trait in the history of borderlands. Sudden upsurges in cross-border flows of goods, people, and capital are known to trigger chronic interstate contentions over territorial sovereignty and border location. The complex relation between territorial disputes, militarised conflict, and economic integration has attracted a great deal of scholarly attention and controversy (e.g. Vasquez and Henehan 2001, Simmons 2005; Vasquez 2009) especially when it comes to conflict and trade (e.g Morrow 1999; Mansfield and Pollins, eds. 2003; Hegre et al. 2010). The problem of missing and noisy data on trade flows represents, as Kenneth A. Schultz aptly points out, "not just a nuisance to be fixed but a manifestation of the phenomenon of interest, since a poorly functioning border regime makes it harder to accurately monitor and report cross-border flows" (2015, 127-128). Jurisdictional and political uncertainties bedevil cross-border economic activities, regardless of actual conflict among the states sharing the border(s). The risks associated with unclear rights over contested territories determine higher transaction costs, discouraging investments and financial ventures. The higher the costs of legitimate channels, the stronger the incentive to use alternative, unauthorised ones.

While displays of military muscle and appeals to commercial peace vie for public opinion, illegal cross-border trade thrives in the trans-Himalayan regions. The contested status of the Sino-Indian border, with its troubled history of contacts, trade, and migration, makes of this "liminal" region an ideal site to investigate the chronological evolution of illegal economies. The informal institutions

---

[1] https://timesofindia.indiatimes.com/india/india-china-troops-clash-at-naku-la-in-sikkim-injuries-on-both-sides/articleshow/80444001.cms (online, updated on January 25, 2021).
[2] https://telecom.economictimes.indiatimes.com/news/huawei-bags-rs-300-crore-network-contract-from-bharti-airtel/81353839 (online, updated on March 6, 2021).

presently active along the Silinguri corridor, a 22-kilometre-wide slice of Indian land sandwiched between Nepal, Bhutan, and Bangladesh, represent the legacy of deeply entrenched smuggling networks. To gain a better understanding of the current border tensions and the way in which conflict, trade, and illegal activities affect and interact with other, a wider, diachronic and more ethnically inclusive perspective is therefore needed.

The present work aims to contribute to the discourse on illegality/illicitness in the trans-Himalayan borderlands by examining the activities of local agents, especially Tibetans, in the area of Kalimpong, West Bengal between the mid-1930s and early 1960s. Spanning from the Great Depression to the Sino-Indian war of 1962, these three decades witnessed the emergence and development of informal exchange networks, endowed with a remarkable resilience despite their localised, fragmented, and ephemeral structure.

The study opens with an overview of the relevant literature in borderland studies in general, and of illicit flows across international borders in particular. After reviewing the main arguments and findings, I will introduce Kalimpong as a case-study to postulate the existence of a complex and often ambivalent relation between border porosity, state trade regulations and enforcement, and border economies. The history of the trade hub is presented as indicative of the gap existing between "legality" and "legitimacy" in regions where the dealings and movements of ethnic and kin networks transgress nation-state laws and regulations. The plasticity of such social organisations in face of national and supranational events and policy changes allows them to compete with global commodity chains, thus creating alternative channels for production, exchange, delivery, and consumption, as we shall see in the following pages.

A change in scale is often required in order to fully appreciate the way in which illicit border economies impact state ones. Following the chronological course of events, I will adjust the frame of reference, alternatively zooming in and out. Sometimes I will scale down from the level of the nation-state (e.g. India, China) to examine the way local actors reacted and adapted to exogenous and endogenous factors; sometimes I will scale up to embrace a wider, global view (e.g. WWI, WWII); and sometimes I will scale across to expose interethnic collusions at the core of many illegal exchange networks. The globalising power of crime in face of state-led attempts at control and repression arguably constitutes an asset of such informal institutions, despite the volatility of interethnic collaborations vis-à-vis ethnic solidarities. The building up of tensions and consequent outbursts of violence will be assessed against law enforcement and state forbearance, exposing the delicate social balance upon which the borderlands rested.

The picture that emerges from this study is that of a system of informal institutions largely inchoate and, as such, extremely adaptable. In the late 1920s and early 1930s, the monetary crisis caused by the Great Depression determined an upsurge of counterfeit coins smuggled from West Bengal to Tibet via Kalimpong. Traditional exchange channels were revitalised, and smuggling became deeply integrated with regional informal economies. The success of such illegal networks much relied on their social licitness, that is to say, their acceptability in the eyes of those involved in them, either directly (e.g. porters, fencers, dealers) or indirectly (e.g. local residents, complicit policemen). Whereas drug smuggling and sex trafficking never enjoyed the social protection necessary to thrive, especially among the Tibetans, other dealings fared much better. That was the case of the dutiable goods that were contrabanded in great number across the border in wartime, when global political uncertainties and trade restrictions contributed to make of the trans-Himalayan borderlands a site ripe with possibilities.

In the 1950s, Asia's post-war settlement, with its major political and economic shifts, heavily affected the sensitive trans-Himalayan borderlands. The Independence of India first (1947) and the establishment of China's People Republic later (1949) took place in a wider context of economic

2

stagnation and hyperinflation that impacted formal and informal economies alike. Generally speaking, the variety of goods that illegally found their way across the border responded to market rationales: while in the late 1920s and early 1930s counterfeit coins were syphoned northbound to dampen the monetary crisis investing Tibet, in wartime the request of supplies from the Chinese front redirected the illegal flows towards specific classes of goods (e.g. food grains, cotton, weapons). Likewise, in the aftermath of WWII, Tibet's need for hard currency clashed with India's blunt refusal to release any substantial amount of foreign currency. Contrary to the official understanding of the situation as reported in archival documents and lately reproduced by several scholars (e.g. Goldstein 1989), India's reluctance was not prompted by a resentment over territorial claims, rather by the financial difficulties that the government was experiencing.

The political changes occurring at a supranational level determined a surge in the illegal flows of goods as well as people. Following China's encroachment on Tibet in 1950, Kalimpong registered a significant rise in criminal activities and private violence. Tibetan vagrants crossed the border in growing numbers, adding strain to the already fragile social balance of the area. Dispossessed, disenfranchised, and with no citizenship, these undocumented immigrants fell through the cracks of the system, thus contributing to the emergence of a general feeling of instability and unsafety.

The study continues by scrutinising the socio-political consequences of the Sino-Indian treaty of 1954. The lack of references to the sensitive issue of border delimitations opened the door to dangerous ambiguity over territorial rights. The growing tension between the superpowers rose to a breaking point in 1962: the border war ended with China's unilateral declaration of ceasefire and its withdrawal behind the LAC, where it remains to this day.

The ensuing closure of the border leads me to the conclusive part of my research, in which I will reflect on the resilience of illicit/illegal networks in the face of political and economic strains, and on the fate of those Tibetans who had tried to live astride two worlds and who instead ended up being lost in the "peripheral hinterland of two irreconcilable civilizations" (Rawat 2004, as quoted in Smyer Yü 2018, 12).

Much of the fascination surrounding illicit flows derives from their being hidden in plain sight. In the borderlands, smuggling is a sin that has no sinner, as social legitimacy extends protection to anyone involved in the "trade". Historical research on trans-Himalayan illicit economies is not necessarily inaccurate, but it is certainly incomplete. This work picks up from previous scholarship on the topic to suggest a more complex picture, in which border economies are integrated into the wider context of national, supranational, and global ones, and the informal institutions embedded in them considered against issues of nation-state's attempts at political legitimacy. To do so, I call on the research of many scholars of border dynamics, informal and criminal economy, and history of global Asia, building my investigation of primary sources upon their insights.

Records of illegal activities in the trans-Himalayan borderlands is rather patchy. Information is scattered and partial, and the study of the subject is often one of silences and voids. Piercing the veil requires framing the available sources into a dialectal relationship, bridging the gaps through constructive juxtapositions. Archival documents (i.e. official notes and dispatches, department files and constitutional assembly's debates, intercepted telegrams and legal verdicts) are here presented in their entirety to better appreciate the colonial and post-colonial language in relation to cross-border (il)licitness.

Since Nicholas B. Dirk's ground-breaking critique of the archive (2002), historians know better than to take archival sources at face value.[3] The "facts" and "truths" produced by the archives are not

---

[3] For a critique of colonial archives, see, among others, Stoler (2002, 2009).

"neutral", rather they reflect bureaucratical categories and processes, since "the state literally produces, adjudicates, organizes, and maintains the discourses that become available as the primary texts of history" (Dirk 2002, 58). By its own nature, the archive is "simultaneously the outcome of historical process and the very condition for the production of historical knowledge" (Dirk 2002, 48), and as such it becomes a default repository of a pre-construed rhetoric of rule. This is even truer for those non-colonial subjects who were, nevertheless, imperial ones, as convincingly argued by Carole Mcgranahan (2017) in the case of Tibetans active in India under the British Raj.

In the following paragraphs, I will amply draw from both British and Indian archives to uncover the way the state apparatus – either imperial or republican – digested and filed any illegal occurrences at its borders. In an effort to balance the state-centric perspective of the archive, the official materials will be corroborated by contemporary newspapers, most of which drafted in Tibetan for a Tibetan readership. For quite a long time, scholars have tended to shy away from any use of the press, grossly considered to be, to use Glenn. R. Wilkinson's brilliant metaphor, "the lignite of the historical world rather than the anthracite" (1995, 211). Newspapers were, in other words, judged by some to be mines of information, but of trivial character – coal rather than gold pits. Yet, since the late 1980s, modern scholarship has gradually overcome such a prejudice and the press has been legitimised as source of scholarly inquiry. In contexts where official records are inaccessible, contemporary journals and magazines may be the only primary source available to historians to reconstruct past events and possibly gauge the public reception of them. The latter part comes with a *caveat* though: newspapers differ in form and content, and so do their intended readership. To expect to size up the "mood" of a society by the tone of its press would require an extensive quantitative and qualitative scrutiny, as a representative sample of newspapers, journals, and magazines ought to be examined. In the case in question, figures are not in our favour: in the Tibetan world, the printed word "was always an object of reverence and less a medium of mass communication" (Erhard 2015, 155), and, of the earliest attempts at secular media, regrettably few are available for close investigation. Among these, a preeminent place is occupied by *The Mirror of News from All Sides of the World* (*Yul phyogs so so'i gsar 'gyur me long*) – hereafter, the *Tibet Mirror* – a Tibetan-language newspaper printed in Kalimpong by Dorje Tharchin (rDo rje mThar phyin, 1890-1976) between 1925 and 1963.[4] Out of approximately 140 issues, 97 – about seventy percent of the newspaper's full run – have been digitised and made available online by Columbia University.

The relevance of the *Tibet Mirror* in the present discussion primarily lies in its place of production: aside from news of global character, Tharchin's newspaper contains numerous references to local events animating the hill station, thus consigning to print names and facts that would have been otherwise forgotten, and it does so through the medium of the Tibetan written word. The relevance of the last point should not be dismissed: most of the documents that will be presented in this article were produced in a mainly Anglophone world, be it that of the British Raj or of post-Independence India. Here, Tibetans figure as extras, background characters that fall flat on the sheets, their existence being of interest only in relation to other, more important factors: colonial affairs, national suzerainty, public security.[5] Dorje Tharchin's accounts, on the contrary, dig deeper and unearth their names, their origins,

---

[4] For more information on the *Tibet Mirror* and its reception, see, among others, Shakya (2004, 18-23), Engelhardt (2011), Holmes-Tagchungdarpa (2014), Erhard (2015), Sawerthal (2018). On the figure of Babu Tharchin in general, and his intelligence-gathering activities in particular, see Fader (2002) and Sen (2021).

[5] The nature of the archive as both repository of documents and primary document of history cautions against an uncritical reading of it. The "facts" and "truths" produced by the archives are not "neutral", rather they reflect categories and processes that "the state literally produces, adjudicates, organizes, and maintains the discourses that become available as the primary texts of history" (Dirk 2002, 58). For a critique of colonial

and, sometimes, the motives behind their actions. Whereas other sources, including official ones such as department files or constitutional assembly's debates, focus on the act (e.g. smuggling), the *Tibet Mirror* brings into the picture the actors – smugglers, petty traders, local dealers – thus escaping the strictures of nation-state's interpretations in favour of a localised, micro-oriented perception of the phenomena in question.[6]

Illegal economies and borderlands. The case of Kalimpong

Illegal economies are commonly conceived as ungoverned, "underground" (Witte, Eakin and Simon 1982), "shadow" (Schneider and Enste 2000), "hidden" and "under the radar of the state" (Oviedo, Thomas and Karakurum-Özdemir 2009), and as such assumed to be regulated exclusively through informal clientelistic institutions, often operating under the forbearance of the state (Tendler 2002; Holland 2015, 2016). Amongst the plethora of phenomena that fall under the label of "criminal activities", many seek to use geographical remoteness as a means to escape state control: such "black economies" in fact need invisibility to succeed (van Schendel and Abraham 2005, 23). Treated for a long time as "margins of the states, societies, economies and culture" (van Schendel 2005, 44), borderlands appear to be naturally intertwined with illicitness. Weak state institutions, ensconced clientelistic networks, and distance from central authority all concur to make of these "ungoverned" and often "ungovernable" territories the ideal setting for all kinds of criminal activities.

More than twenty years ago, in urging a departure from the traditional "vision from the centre", Michiel Baud and Willem van Schendel argued for the adoption of new theoretical frames to borderlands – some novel analytical approaches that, in escaping the centripetal force of the state as a centre of gravity, allowed "for a view from the periphery" (1997, 212). Since then, border studies have increasingly emancipated themselves from state-centrism, further elaborating on the concepts of "borderlands" and "frontiers" as both socio-historical and spatial categories.[7] As Tobias Wendl and Michael Rösler remind us,

> Our world is made up of borders and frontiers. [...] As barriers they repel, as transitions they attract and disclose dynamic interstitial zones of "no more" and "not yet", yet also of "as well", cristallization points of multiculturalism, intercultural contact and crossover. (1999, 1)

It is in such an "in-betweenness" (Wendl and Rösler 1999, 1), where political, cultural, and social identities fuse and friction, coexist and conflict, that moral and legal notions of (il)licitness and (il)legality fade and intersect. Regardless of dissimilar historical conditions that determined the emergence and development of their territories, all borderlanders share a deep-rooted awareness of the crossovers and dualities etched in the multipolar environment they inhabit, a phenomenon that the historian Oscar Martinez calls "the border experience" (1994, xviii).[8] The common structural setting of the border – that the nation-state ideology would want fixed and stable – escapes those very same

---

archives, see, among others, Dirk (2002) and Stoler (2009). On the "troubled" and "troubling" categorisation of Tibetans in the British colonial archives, see, in particular, McGranahan (2017).

[6] As any other newspaper, the *Tibet Mirror* is also afflicted by a biased perspective: Babu Tharchin's patrons in fact included the Scottish Mission (for the years 1925-1931 and 1932-1946), the British Raj (for the years 1942-1948), the Government of India (1948-1949), and even the Tibetan government, although the latter's contributions were rather sporadic. In the light of that, the content of the *Tibet Mirror* tended towards Christian proselytism and pro-British positions. See Sawerthal (2018).

[7] See, among others, Baud and van Schendel (1997),Wendl and Rösler (1999), Donnan and Wilson (1999, 2012), Hall (2005), Rodseth and Parker (2005) Parker (2006), Hämäläinen and Truett (2011), Johnson et al. (2011), Rumford (2012), van Schendel and de Maaker (2014), Imamura (2015).

[8] The term "border" is here used in conformity with Baund and van Schendel's definition of "political divides that were the result of state building, especially from the eighteenth century onward" (1997, 214).

topdown strictures, thus exposing an inherent porosity much subject to "the similarity of the countries adjoined [by the border], the symmetry of the dominant crossing patterns and, finally, the historical context in which a particular border has developed its dynamics and permeability" (Wendl and Rösler 1999, 9). The ever-shifting balance between these parameters creates transient and translocal borderlands, temporary and spatially differentiated by degrees of central control, local penetrability, and social fluidity.[9] The openness or closure of borders heavily affects the life of the communities in the surrounding regions, directing cross-national flows and segmenting regulatory spaces, carving niches of social licitness wherein illegal activities are tolerated if not openly incentivised. Black market, smuggling, counterfeit, prostitution, and trafficking thrive in "grey areas" – remote zones, literally or figuratively, where central control is weak, and the balance of local powers asymmetrical. To borrow from Sven Tägil and colleagues, "boundaries separate people (or groups of people) and the separating qualities of boundaries influence interactions between them" (1977, 14): in other words, the level of permeability of a border determines the organisation of local and translocal relationships.

In terms of illegal economies, both sides of the border spectrum – total closure and total openness – impact negatively on the locally active, routinised, informal regulatory structures. At one end, a closed border creates "alienated" borderlands, wherein tension and conflict prevail, and illegal economies are run by large institutional organisations (Gallien 2018, 4), de facto cutting small players off. At the other end, a totally open border conversely generates "integrated" borderlands, where similar economic conditions across the border allow for virtually unrestricted movement and exchange, thus nullifying any payoffs that engaging in illegal trading activities may yield.[10] For illegal economies to prosper, therefore, the border must be porous but only up to a point: the states on both sides of the boundary line must coexist and be interdependent, yet a certain degree of asymmetry in economic conditions and crossing patterns must occur for locals to act as cultural brokers specialised in transborder business and affair (Wendl and Rösler 1999, 10).

National borders are a relatively recent political construct: many premodern societies lacked clearly defined territorial states, and no connections were drawn between a government and the ethnic, cultural, and linguist unity of its people. Pluralist political units, such as empires, presented a hierarchical power structure, in which a "core" region ruled over a diversified and virtually autonomous periphery. The concept of nation-state, based on the notion that "states should be governed in the name of a nationally defined community of equal citizen" (Wimmer and Min 2006, 874) was largely an exception in global governance as late as the 19th century.

In the light of that, it is hardly surprising that the same terms "frontier", "boundary", and "borderland" are still the object of dispute in the anglophone academic community. Generally speaking, the word "frontier" carries with it an idea of "emptiness" and "wilderness" to be conquered and civilised: a space where territorial claims may be laid, and processes of inclusion/exclusion alternatively enacted and contested. Once a boundary is drawn and a border set, the regions on either sides of it become, patently, "borderlands", here understood to be both the areas in a nation that are significantly affected by the border and the dividing line between two different peoples and cultures.

---

[9] On the changing of borders over space and time, see in particular Baud and van Schendel (1997).

[10] The first to propose a four-model categorisation of borderlands was Oscar Martínez (1994), who frames his discourse in terms of "alienation" (no routine cross-border interactions), "coexistence" (minimum cross-border interactions), "interdependence" (high level of cross-border interactions), and "integration" (no barriers to trade and human flows across the border). For the sake of convenience, these models have been here used as heuristic tools for comparing borderlands, with the due *caveat* that any locally specific social, political, and economic dimensions will inevitably fail to be registered into such gross approximations.

Where two or more powers come into contact, frontiers emerge and sometimes clash, leading to what Baud and van Schendel define as "embryonic borderlands" (1997, 223).[11] The temporal and spatial developments of borderland regions have significant repercussions on the overlapping political, social, and cultural networks that enliven them. Such "transboundary social formations" (Herrog 1990, 135) connect state(s), regional elites, and local populace in a triangulation of powers that are in constant flux. The hypersensitivity of borderlands to global events contributes to make such a balance of relationships prone to sudden changes: international trade agreements may cause economically depressed regions to thrive unexpectedly, only to lose any financial and cultural advantage in the aftermath of an interstate war and the subsequent closure of the border. That was indeed the case for many areas in Northern South Asia, the subregion proposed by David Gellner to label the geographic space enclosed by "India's mainly mountainous northern borders" (2013, 1).[12]

Natural demarcation separating the Indian subcontinent from the Tibetan plateau, the Himalayas still represented for the late 19th- and early 20th-century British colonial officers "a God-given boundary set to [a] vast, impressive and stupendous frontier" (Holdich 1901, 280).[13] Yet, despite any Western romantic notions of inviolability, the Himalayan ranges were crossed by several traversable passages the existence of which had been known to local populations for centuries. A theatre of migration, travel, and trade, the valleys on either side of the "border" both suffered and profiteered from colonial territorial conquest and mapping first, and postcolonial imposition of those same maps and boundaries later.

The borderland nature of the regions separated by the Himalayas, and the interconnectivity of the people living in them, have been the object of many recent studies.[14] In the late 18th and early 19th centuries, the global affirmation of nation-states' sovereignty and fixed borders disrupted the traditional

---

[11] Anastasia Piliavsky convincingly argues against a blanket application of the concept of borderlands to regions around national borders, drawing attention to the relational rather than substantive essence of borders. According to her, "[borders] generate different sorts of relations within and between communities around them" (2013, 27) and various features assumed to be distinctive markers of borderlands, such as a synthetic language and culture, collusions between state officials and local elites or illegal economies, are actually present in the heartlands as well. Piliavsky is not the first to have noticed the consequences of global migration, displacement, and urban agglomerations: as early as 1999, the four-model theory proposed by Martínez (1994) and adopted by Baud and van Schendel (1997) was partially revised by Wendl and Rösler to include "figurative multi-sited borderlands", which "are neither spatially bounded nor do they have a particular location within national center-periphery frames" (1999, 10). A similar approach has been more recently suggested by the historian Tagliacozzo (2005) in his study of smuggling along the Southeast Asian frontier. While reconstructing the nature of illicit traffic in the region, he correctly links the phenomenon with specific locales, all sharing common peculiarities, namely that of being "blind spots", invisible to the state's eyes. In his own words, "[u]ndertrading as a category in history happens most often in three places: at borders and peripheries, furthest from the vision and reach of the state; at natural choke points, such as mountain passes and narrow waterways, where trade is channeled because of geography; and in urban confusion, where the state is somewhat blinded by the frenzy of activity" (2005, 5). Be that as it may, borderlands still seem to escape clear-cut definitions and remain contested ground for border theorists. For the sake of convenience, I am here mainly adopting Baud and van Schendel's approach to borderlands as a heuristic tool.

[12] According to Gellner, the term was firstly used by Hiroshi Ishii, Katsuo Nawa, and himself in two edited volumes published in 2007. For bibliographical references, see Gellner (2013).

[13] The notion of the Himalayas as "a political frontier as well as a scientific frontier" (Arnold 2014, 200) was very much present in British East India Company's efforts to develop a trade route connecting India to China via Tibet.

[14] See, among others, Smyer Yü and Michaud (2018), Harris (2017a), Vasantkumar (2017), Moran and Warner (2016), and Gellner (2013). Relevant, especially in respect to illicitness and illegality at the borders, is Scott (2009). Although controversial and partially revisited by Scott himself, the notion of Zomia and, in particular, his idea of "non-state spaces" located beyond the state's influence remain two useful investigative tools to engage with borderlanders' forms of state evasion. On licit and illicit trading networks in the Tibetan world, see in particular van Spengen (2000).

cultural, religious, and trade networks connecting the different communities across the mountain ranges: new regulated ports of entry and exit emerged, and borders became sites of contestation and dispute, where legal and illegal economies intermingled and overlapped (2005, 48).

In discussing illegal/illicit flows and borders, Willem van Schendel (2005) structures his argument through dichotomous categories, drawing attention to invisibility and mobility as core features of illegal economies: smugglers, counterfeiters, and dealers are, by the definition, drifting, shady, and inconspicuous.[15] They are, in many cases, disenfranchised, either by choice or force; that was indeed the case for most of the Tibetans operating in the area of Kalimpong.

The history of Kalimpong has been, in many ways, one of exchanges. Originally part of Sikkim, the land strip lying eastwards of the Teesta River was annexed by Bhutan in 1706, only to be sold to the British a century and a half later, in the aftermath of the Anglo-Bhutanese war. At the time of its annexation to British India in 1865, Kalimpong was nothing more than a hamlet located within a scarcely populated area, mainly inhabited by Lepcha and Bhotia communities (Viehbeck 2017, 3).[16] In a period when hill stations such as Darjeeling were objects of colonial investment as therapeutic leisure resorts and tea plantations (Sharma 2016), Kalimpong emerged primarily as an agrarian zone, able to attract farmers and labourers from nearby Nepal (Viehbeck 2017, 3) as well as numerous merchants and peddlers headed to its lively market. Already connected to the long-distance trade routes that criss-crossed Central, South, and Southeast Asia, in the early 20th century Kalimpong developed into a main node of economic and cultural cross-border exchanges, gradually morphing into a space of encounters or, to follow Markus Viehbeck's approach, a "contact zone".[17]

By the late 19th century, "a few huts and two or three families with eight cows" (Rennie 1866, 21, as quoted in Majumdar 1993, 574) had turned into a village-sized settlement: the colonial power quickly realised the potentialities of Kalimpong, as did the Christian missionaries. The Church of Scotland Mission opened the first Primary School in 1873, less than a decade after the annexation, and other establishments mushroomed in the following years; by 1900, a large missionary settlement had spread over the hill slopes to the northeast of the main village. In the following years, Kalimpong became a centre for elite education: its boarding schools, fashioned on the British model, hosted the offspring of the better off, be they British, Anglo-Indians or foreigners.[18]

---

[15] Historical sources documenting illicit activities are, by and large, fragmentary and elusive, and often unable to provide more than a one-sided viewpoint, especially in colonial contexts. Particularly valuable are therefore the in-depth studies by Tagliacozzo (2005) and Thai (2018) on the interaction between smuggling and state(s) along the Anglo-Dutch frontier in Southeast Asia (1865-1915) and the Chinese coast (1842-1965) respectively. See also the thematic volumes edited by Gros (2016, 2019) for a study of the Sino-Tibetan borderlands between the 18th and the 20th centuries.

[16] Both Lepchas and Bhotias (alternative spelling, Bhutias, Bhootias, or Bhotiyas) are resident tribes of Sikkim. Also known as Rong, the Lepchas perceive themselves as autochthones, although their indigeneity is still matter of debate in western anthropological discourse. Less controversial is the origin of the Bhotias, who migrated from Eastern Tibet to Sikkim in the 14th century (Arora 2007). Denoting the people of the area of Bhot, the term Bhotia is etymologically related to the late Sanskrit *bhotah*, itself a loan word from the Tibetan *bod*, "Tibet" (Ramble 1993). The popularisation of Bhotia as an ethnic category occurred between the 18th and 19th centuries, when the diverse range of Tibetan-speaking Buddhist communities encountered by the British Empire in its expansion from Bengal to the western Himalayas via Nepal were progressively grouped under the same label. For a detailed discussion on the trade, identity, and mobility of the Bhotias, see Bergmann (2016).

[17] The term "contact zone", introduced in early 1990s by Marie Louise Pratt "to refer to social spaces where cultures meet, clash, and grapple with each other, often in contexts of highly asymmetrical relations of power, such as colonialism, slavery, or their aftermaths" (1991, 34), is adopted by Viehbeck as a conceptual framework to interpret the historical developments of Kalimpong in light of power dynamics, entanglements, transculturation/transculturality, and contact (2017, 7-13).

[18] Neither a traditional trade node nor a strategic locale for British interests, Kalimpong's development into a town was largely due the efforts of Rev. William McFarlane, a missionary of the Church of Scotland, who

In the aftermath of the Younghusband Expedition (1903-1904), trade – begun in earnest after the Anglo-Chinese Trade Convention (1893)[19] and the subsequent opening of a British mart at Yatung – increased dramatically, and with it did the flows of people, goods, and knowledge passing through the area: Kalimpong was by then a major hub along the Lhasa-Calcutta route (Majumdar 1993; Viehbeck 2017; Sherpa 2019). The development of Kalimpong as a hill station has been examined in detail elsewhere (Majumdar 1993, 2006), and need not to be repeated here. New settlement areas were created, and the original tenants – Lepchas, Bhotias, and Nepalese – were relocated to make room for newcomers, mostly Anglo-Indians, Bengalis, Europeans, but also wealthy Tibetans who in numbers were renting housing and business spaces. By the 1920s, the process of urbanisation was completed (Majumdar 1993); recognised as a town in 1931, Kalimpong became a municipality fourteen years later (Viehbeck 2017, 5).

Fuelled by a booming economic growth, in the first part of the 20th century the hill station became a multicultural melting pot, where identity was created and negotiated, different networks interacted and overlapped, and boundaries were crossed, both literally and figuratively. The border with Tibet, which prior to the Younghusband Expedition had been formally closed for two centuries by the Qing, was now a territory of exchange and vibrant activity. Trade along the Lhasa-Calcutta route had a main centre of distribution in Kalimpong: here goods in transit were stored, unpacked, checked, sorted, and relocated through various formal and informal channels. Legal trade corridors, regulated by permits and quotas and subject to taxation and security clearance, were flanked by other passageways, the nature of which was informal and self-enforced "through mechanisms of obligations, such as in patron-client relationships or clan networks, or simply because following the rules [was] in the best interests of individuals who may find themselves in a situation in which everyone [was] better off through co-operation" (de Soysa and Jütting 2007, 31).

Contrary to the assumptions of mainstream political science, which subsumes illegal economies underneath the conceptual umbrella of informal institutions and as such characterised by small-scale organisational units, little third-party engagement, and personalised relationships of exchange, many activities performed within an "illegal" framework actually straddle multiple levels of regulation, as shown by recent scholarship of illegal economies (Webb, et al. 2009; Titeca and Flynn 2010; Beckert and Dewey 2017). Formal and informal institutions do, in other words, interact constantly and they do so within culturally defined norms and beliefs, the same that determine the nature of economic activity (de Soysa and Jütting 2007, 32).

When dealing with borderlands economies, the concepts of (il)legality and (il)licitness necessarily come to the fore. When a gap exists between what is "legal" according to law and regulations and what is deemed "licit" by norms, values, and beliefs (Webb, et al. 2009, 492), illegal economies may emerge. Positioned as they are at the fringes of the state, borderlands are the perfect terrain for ongoing struggles over legitimacy: here personal interests clash, and licit and illicit practices coexist in social life and overlap in state processes. The same definition of what the state deems "illicit" (i.e. illegal) is in fact situational, as it changes accordingly with political, social, and economic conditions (van Schendel and Abraham 2005) – a case particularly evident when cross-border flows, be

---

established the first church and school here. On the role played by the Mission in making Kalimpong a centre of Western education and medicine, see McKay (2007, 55-78).

[19] Better known as "Regulations Regarding Trade, Communication and Pasturage", it was meant to be appended to the Anglo-Chinese Convention Relating to Sikkim and Tibet signed in 1890.

they of commodities or people, are taken into consideration.[20] As Willem van Schendel and Itty Abraham point out,

> We need to approach flows of goods and people as visible manifestations of power configurations that weave in and out of legality, in and out of states, and in and out of individuals' lives, as socially embedded, sometimes long-term processes of production, exchange, consumption, and representation. (2005, 9)

Commodity chains, at a national and global level, are heavily affected by illegal economies, which can compete with or even substitute segments of the chain, thus creating alternative pathways for commodities to be produced, exchanged, delivered or consumed. In the following pages, Kalimpong will emerge both as a vital node in the distributing network connecting Calcutta to Lhasa and as a centre of local production and consumption of products of illegal origin.

Illegality in the 1930s: coining wealth at the borders

In the earliest months of 1933, an arrest made news in the relatively quiet hill station of Kalimpong. From the April issue of the *Tibet Mirror*:

> Counterfeit of rupees and Tibetan coins in Kalimpong: around April 11, the chief of the Kalimpong police checked the shop of the trader Morsingh Kalyan in Kalimpong where there were large iron pliers to make four kinds of Indian coins – silver coin rupees of 4 anna, 2 anna, and 1 anna – and Tibetan silver *sho*.[21] The pliers' heads were engraved on both right and left [sides] to strike the head and tail of the *sho* [coin]. In the middle, a resistant, hard [piece] of copper *sho* [= here intended as weight ~ 1.2 tola/ 14 gr] was inserted. When pressed together, a copy of a *sho* would likely come out. The four types of Indian coins were realised in a more delicate way, as they were poured [into a cast]. Two Indian minters and Kalyan had been arrested. Shortly, they will be tried in court. Since most of the rupees that had been coined [bore] the year 1919, the traders must pay attention. [These] evil, creative people have coined a large quantity of rupees and Tibetan coins; no one can guess how many of them circulate now.[22]

---

[20] To echo Tagliacozzo, there is no ontology to the category of contraband, as "contraband [is] whatever those in power [say] it [is], and these designations sometimes [change] very quickly" (2005, 65).

[21] As late as the 17th century, Tibet had no currency. Trade was carried out either on a barter basis or through ingots of silver and gold. Between the 1640s and 1792, the coinage circulating in Tibet was mainly constituted by silver *mohar*, minted by the Newari kingdoms of Kathmandu, Pātaṇ, and Bhaktapur (Bertsch 2002, 1). In the aftermath of the Gurkha's conquest of the Kathmandu valley in 1769 (Walsh 1973, 23–24; Rhodes et al. 1989, 122; 206), the Tibetan government was forced to cast its own coins. A mint was established in Lhasa in 1791 to be closed only two years later (Rhodes et al. 1989, 206); between 1792 and 1835, the Qing court sponsored the construction and operation of another Lhasa-based mint, but in 1836 the Tibetan government resumed the project of self-minted coinage which had been abandoned in 1794. From 1850, the Indian rupee gained great favour among the Tibetan traders, up to the point of being the only currency to be used in Eastern Tibet. Between 1903 and 1911, the Chinese government endeavoured to reduce the economic predominance of the Indian rupee by issuing a coin struck in Sichuan (i.e. the Sichuan rupee), which gained some degree of popularity among the traders active on the Sino-Tibetan border. The Tibetan government, in an attempt to free its economy from the influence exerted by both the Chinese and the Indian currencies, actively sustained the local production of coins and banknotes. The Indian rupee however managed to maintain some value among the traders who travelled south to the markets of Kalimpong and India, while the Sichuan rupee gradually lost its appeal and became insignificant by the 1950s. The last coins to be struck under Tibetan authority date to 1954, while the last banknotes were issued in 1959; since then, the Chinese renminbi has become the currency in use in Tibet. Tibetan coins were categorised as *khagang* (*kha gang*), *karma* (*skar ma*), *karchegye* (*skar phyed brgyad*), *tamka* (*ṭam ka*), *sho* (*zho*), *sang* (*srang*), *dotse* (*rdo tshad*). The different nomenclatures introduced in the above passage were subdivisions within a complex currency system practically based on silver *sang*, or *ngülsang* (*dngul srang*). The system followed a decimal base, as the each *sang* was equivalent to 10 *sho*, which in turn was equal to 10 *karma*. The *dotse* held the highest value of 50 *sang* (Bertsch 2002, 4-5).

[22] *ka sbug tu dbyin sgor dang bod dngul rdzus ma bzo 'dug || ka sbug rgya gar tshong pa mor sing kan ya'i tshong khang la ka sbug pu li si dpon pos dbyin zla 5 [*4] ta rig 11 nyin skor nas nang btsal song bas | der dbyin gzhung dngul sgor mo a na 4 | a na 2 | a na 1 bcas rnam pa bzhi bzos pa dang | bod gzhung dngul zho gang*

The nature of the crime was not such as to attract the morbid attention of Babu Tharchin's readership, yet counterfeiting was undoubtedly cause of concern among the local dwellers. Heavy sentences were often converted into lighter ones, a relaxation of the penalty that increased the perceived risk of repetition of offences. An update to a previous case, reported in the following issue of the *Tibet Mirror* dated May 1933, appears to suggest a certain common anxiety shared by the Tibetan residents of Kalimpong, most of whom were at the time involved in the trade business.

> In a past issue (year 2, number 9) dated 1st day of the 7th month of the Fire Hare Year [August 28, 1927], it was reported that a Nepalese man called Birkharaj was arrested and sentenced to eight years of jail time for counterfeiting Tibetan *sho* and [Indian] *paisa*. After being immediately imprisoned, his sentence was reduced, and now he is back in Kalimpong. Eight years have yet to go by, still it seems that the government looked at him with kindness and [his punishment] was quite reduced.[23]

Counterfeit belies the receptivity of borderlands to cross-border socio-economic factors. In the late 1920s and early 1930s, with the Great Depression hitting the global markets hard, Tibet was facing a monetary crisis of its own, triggered by large numbers of counterfeit copper coins freely circulating in the country (Lin 2006, 54). The Himalayan hill stations were the pointed of entry for the forged money that, funnelled through the southeastern border, penetrated the Tibetan market.[24] In the late 1920s, Calcutta was a main centre of counterfeit money production: Tibetan copper coins (*sho*), freshly minted in one of the illegal workshops of the city, were funnelled to Darjeeling and Kalimpong through a network of complacent agents, Indians, Nepalese, and Tibetans alike. Nicholas Rhodes' study (1992) offers precious information on such a widespread, yet little documented phenomenon. Based on private files and physical evidences kept by his wife's grandfather S. W. Laden La,[25] at the time Additional Superintendent of the police in Darjeeling, Rhodes reconstructs the criminal case reported in the *Tibet Mirror*, providing more details on the matter.

Rumours of counterfeit copper *sho*, manufactured in Calcutta for the Tibetan market, reached Laden La's ears in early December 1925; in the following months, the Superintendent and his team managed to retrace most of the coins to a workshop in Calcutta. A police search of the place, conducted in March 1926, uncovered no evidence, and the only suspect, a certain Jiban Kristo Laha, proved innocent of the charges. The case would have been dropped had it not been for the magnitude of the monetary crisis that hit Tibet that year: in May 1926, the Political Officer in Sikkim, Major F. M. Bailey, was formally requested by the Tibetan Cabinet of Ministers to stop the manufacturing of forged coins

---

bzo byed lcags kyi skam pa chen po 1 bcas 'thon song | skam pa de'i mgo gnyis kyi g.yas g.yon du zho gang gi par rgyab mdun gnyis brkos 'dug | de'i bar zangs zho gang gi sra ba thub bcug ste mnan na zho gang par 'thon gyi yod tshod 'dug | dbyin dngul rnam bzhi 4 rnams 'jam par par brgyab ste blug rgyab kyi yod 'dug | rgya gar bzo pa 2 dang kan yā 1 bcas 'dzin gzung bgyis song | ring min kha mchu khrims kyis zhib dpyod gnang rgyun | sgor mo mang ba 'das lo 1919 pa bzos yod 'dug | de la tshong pa rnams nas blta zhib gnang dgos | mi nang blo chen rnams nas khyon 'bor dbyin bod dngul ga tshod bzos nas btang yod da lta cha ma rtgos || Tibet Mirror 7 (4), 5

[23] *ngon me yos zla 7 tshes 1 gsar 'gyur lo 2 ang 9 nang gsal bod gzhung chen po mchog gi pad sha zho gang brdzus ma bzos skor 'dzin bzung kha mchu thog bal po bhe ka rā dza zer bar lo 8 btson du btang ba de nye lam btson nas lhod yangs byung ste deng ka sbug tu bslebs 'dug | lo brgyad ma 'das kyang gzhung nas brtse gzigs thog lhod ba 'dra || Tibet Mirror 7 (5), 2*

[24] The issue of copper coins in Tibet began in 1909, but it was only four years later, in 1913, with the striking of large numbers of them, that the new coins began to circulate widely as small change (Bertsch and Rhodes 2010, 21).

[25] A Sikkimese Bhotia by birth and Anglophile by belief, S. W. Laden La rose among the ranks of the native agents of the Empire, becoming one of the most renowned figures of the time. Close associate of Sir Charles Bell during his office as Political Officer in Sikkim between 1908 and 1918, he acted as interpreter and diplomat in several occasions. On his life, see Rhodes and Rhodes (2006).

– it was by then public knowledge that the counterfeit *sho* had Indian origins. Bailey forwarded the message to Laden La, who was unable to comply: apparently, most of the copper coins saturating the Tibetan market had been smuggled across the border between 1921 and 1924.

The matter of forgeries continued to be a sore point between British and Tibetan officials, but no positive developments were made throughout 1926. In May 1927 though, while on his way from Darjeeling to Gangtok, Laden La caught sight of a Tibetan leading a group of nine mules: tipped off, the Superintendent stopped the man for questioning, and great was his surprise when the trader declared that he was transporting Tibetan coins. When the loads, eighteen in total, were checked at Rangpo Sikkim Police Outpost, all the money therein contained turned out to be counterfeit *sho*. Similar crates were found in possession of two Nepalese merchants, Naraman Newar and Sherbahadur Newar; when pressed, the three traders confessed to have bought the coins in Calcutta. Set on finding out the mastermind behind the forgeries, Laden La moved the Tibetan, named Tendar (bsTan dar), first to Darjeeling and then to Calcutta; here, with the assistance of the local police, an illegal mint was discovered in the house of another Nepalese trader, the same Birkharaj Newar whose name made news a few months later, when his release was reported in the chronicle section of the *Tibet Mirror*.[26]

The trial was held at the High Court of Calcutta on August 8, 1927, and Birkharaj and five of his accomplices were accused of counterfeiting Tibetan coins and possessing instruments and materials for their manufacture. On August 23, Birkharaj was judged guilty of coin and banknote forgery and condemned to six years for the first charge and two for the second one. As we have seen, things did not play out as expected, and less than six years later, in early 1933, the Nepalese was discharged.

Rhodes' highly informative article contains the full statement of Tendar as it was given to Landen La at the time of his arrest. For the sake of the present discussion, I will here present a brief excerpt as indicative of the interplay of legal and illegal economies in social life.

> [...] Narman Newar informed me that there is a Newar who is selling copper coins made in Calcutta. I enquired what kind of coins. He showed me one which was like the Tibetan *Sho* coins which are in circulation in Tibet. Narman suggested that it would be better for us to purchase such coins and sell in Tibet on double profit. Then I went to the house of that Newar near Bara Bazar. His name is Birkharaj or Birkhare Newar. There were three other Newars in the house who were all manufacturing *Sho* copper coins. Birkharaj [...] showed us how the coins are manufactured. We then bargained the price and it was decided that he would sell us the coins at Rs. 3/8/- per hundred *Sho* coins. [...] Birkharaj told us that he would make all arrangements for packing the coins so that no Tibetan or British officials can suspect their contents during transit. On his request we shifted to his house. We lived in the top flat for nearly one and a half months. They manufactured the coins on the ground floor. It has two doors, one facing the road and another back door. It has a partition and the place is so cleverly arranged that outsiders cannot see anything that is going on inside. Birkharaj is a clever man. He brought in some British Police Officers and offered them pan and cigarettes. Whenever any outsider comes to his house, then the door of the working place is always closed. Some Tibetans also visited his house and went away. They did not buy any coins. Birkharaj told me that he sold a large amount of such coins to different Tibetan merchants. Since last year the Tibetan government are watching for such coins, and he advised us not to go towards Phari. Sher Bahadur suggested that we should go to Kampa Dzong (North Sikkim) and travel through Rungpo and Gangtok. This was agreed. I subscribed Rs. 5000/-. Both Narman Newar and Sherbahadur Newar subscribed Rs. 5000/-. We formed a company, and it was decided that all profits and loss will be equally shared. We purchased copper *Sho* coins Rs. 9,500/- and also some brick silver and cloth. [...] (Rhodes 1992, 91)

Unknowing to Tendar, Birkharaj's house becomes, in his statement, a metaphor of the bipolar nature of the people involved in the counterfeit scam: like the two doors of the building – one open on

---

[26] News of Birkharaj's arrest and trial was reported in the *Tibet Mirror* at the time it happened in August 1927. Unfortunately, the issue in question (volume 2, issue 9) was not available to me for consultation.

the front, the other on the back – the forger and his accomplices walked astride two worlds. One out in the open, run by laws and regulations and operating through formal institutions; the other in the shadows, based on codified norms and relying on informal institutions.

Social licitness of illegal flows: smuggling as a "way of border life"

Borderlands may be the centre of production for illegal activities – forged coins are a clear example of that – yet it is in flow dynamics that their innate "in-betweenness" explicates itself best. Border societies use their "'local knowledge' to transform 'state barriers' into corridors for commodities" (Wendl and Rösler 1999, 18), so much so that smuggling becomes "a way of border life" (Driessen 1999),[27] as demonstrated by the case of Kalimpong. Starting from the 1930s illegal imports and exports appeared more and more in the local news and became a hot topic among the British officers first and Indian politicians later.

Small-scale smuggling: drug trafficking in the early 1930s

Reports of Tibetans involved in the smuggling of illegal goods, especially opium, made it to the pages of the *Tibet Mirror* since the early 1930s. In April 1933, a Khampa trader named Kel Nyiga (bsKal nyi dga') and an innkeeper, a certain Norbu (Nor bu), were charged for the import and possession of a *maund* (~ 37 kg) of opium to the value of Rs. 8,000 (*Tibet Mirror* 7 (4), 8); the High Court of Calcutta sentenced Kel Nyiga to one year and Norbu to six months imprisonment.

By the early 20th century, smuggling of Indian opium to China was a known, almost consolidated practice, although mostly confined to maritime trafficking. A lesser-known phenomenon was the production, distribution, and consumption of the drug in the Inner Asian border territories of China, such as Tibet. Far from being an "imported" issue, Inner Asia's drug problem was deeply rooted in the socio-economic fabric of China itself. In his study of the opium market in Qing China, David A. Bello's frame of analysis embraces the entire system, the extent of which "not only encompassed Euro-American coastal traffickers and their Chinese counterparts, but imperial subjects from China proper as well as Inner Asian people living within and just beyond Qing frontiers" (2001, 40). The ethnically distinctive administrative system of the Qing dynasty, with its hybrid, territorially customised organisation, facilitated the diffusion of opium commodity chains beyond China proper.[28]

In the mid-19th century, traffic of opium paste entered Central Tibet by means of the Chinese military personnel stationed in the Lhasa garrison (McKay 2014, 66). Regardless of prohibition statutes issued throughout the 1830s, opium trafficking, cultivation, and consumption remained rampant – addiction among soldiers and accompanying civilians fuelled smuggling and profiteering (Bello 2001, 52-53).[29] By the early 20th century, opium paste was among the illegal commodities that found their

---

[27] To use Tagliacozzo's brilliant metaphor, the dialectic relationship between state and smuggler resembles a waltz – each dancer attuned to their partner's moves and quick to counterbalance them (2005, 373). In such a game, knowledge of local conditions becomes therefore essential (2005, 18), to the point that much of the history of smuggling may be arguably seen as a contest of territorial control.

[28] The drug penetrated China through the Han settlements in Xinjiang: by mid-19th century, locally produced opium poppy flanked Inner Asian varieties, in an attempt to answer the increase in demand (Bello 2001, 50). On the role played by the opium trade in the Turkestan-Xinjiang borderland, see Pianciola (2020).

[29] In 1840, Meng-bao, senior amban in Tibet, notified the court of a series of breaches to the prohibition laws perpetrated in Lhasa by Chinese subjects. Upon investigation, six civilians, all Han Chinese traders and craftsmen connected to the garrison, were charged with opium smoking. Similar accusations were moved by the same Meng-bao towards members of the troops, including a company commander; although found not guilty, all the defendants were cashiered. Most of opium circulating in Tibet in mid-19th century came from domestic production: poppy fields had been discovered in Yunnan (in 1823) and Sichuan (in 1832), and it was from these

way south of the Indian border.[30] In August 1936, several men, among whom figured some Tibetans, were arrested in Kalimpong on charges of drug trafficking:

> [L]ately, from the Sino-Tibetan borderlands, [opium] seems to be arriving in Tibet. After that the local Bureau of Alcohol and Opium had confiscated [opium] arriving in Kalimpong from Tibet in multiple occasions, several people were fined and went to prison. Since opium was produced from the house of Losi-la (Blo si lags), a local citizen, he was imprisoned for six months. An Indian seller of leather shoes was fined 200 rupees. On August 14, 2.5 *sher* (~ 2.3 kg) of opium and [some] barley beer (*chang*) were confiscated from the gathering [place] of Baba-la ('Ba' rba lags) and Nyanya (rNya rnya) in Kalimpong: Baba was sentenced to one year in prison and fined 600 rupees, Nyanya was sentenced to six months in prison and fined 200 rupees, and 215 hard cash silver was confiscated. Yet, they petitioned the Supreme Judge of Darjeeling to investigate [on the matter] again [saying] they were not consuming such poison.[31]

In the late 1930s, both Nationalist China and British India sought to impose a countrywide control over opium distribution: contrary to the harsh statutes issued by the Qing, the Koumintang (KMT) tried to create a monopoly over the entire drug trade, forcing control over the opium shipments along the Yangzi, the fluvial artery connecting the southwestern poppy-growing provinces of Sichuan and Yunnan to the maritime centre of Shanghai. Announced in 1935, Chiang Kai-shek's Six-Year Plan to Eliminate Opium and Drugs aimed to fully eradicate the narcotic by gradually reducing production and authorised consumption while increasing awareness through major propaganda work, registration of addicts, and opening of recovery clinics. By the end of the plan period in April 1940, the KMT declared the campaign of drug control a success, although it was only in 1949, with the establishment of the Communist Party, that poppy cultivations were definitively uprooted.[32]

With its economic reliance on the drug trade on the one hand and enforcement of consumption control on the other, Chiang Kai-shek's plan fell in with the policies adopted in India since the mid-19th century, when a series of acts, with amendments thereto and regulations made thereunder, introduced a complex legislation aimed to control the production, transport, and sale of the drug within the whole of British India.[33] The system of excise administration was lately adopted by the native states, and a series of constitutional changes allowed provincial governments a certain degree of autonomy. Through

---

southwestern provinces that the drug reached Tibet through a trafficking network formed by Han Chinese and "foreigners", most likely Tibetans or some regional ethnic minority (Bello 2001, 51-56).

[30] Until the early 19th century, the drug circulated as a smokable blend known in India as *madak* (Ch. *yapian yan* 鴉片煙, a preparation of opium soaked in a tobacco solution), but by 1813, a new unadulterated opium paste (*yapian yangao* 鴉片煙膏) entered the market with dramatic consequences. Opium paste was highly addictive: the processes of extraction and refinement increased the morphine content up to 9-10%, a substantial enhancement of *madak*'s percentage points, which averaged around 0.2% (Bello 2001, 42).

[31] *[...] deng rgya bod sa mtshams nas bod du yong gi yod tshod | bod nas 'di ga ka sbug tu'ang 'byor gyi yod 'dug pa 'di ga'i tshang rag g.ya' phying [*phyin] las khungs nas 'dzin bzung thengs mang po gnang nas nyes pa dang btson du'ang 'gro mi mang po byung song | nye lam 'di gar gnas pa blo si lags kyi nang nas g.ya' phing [*phyin] thon rkyen zla phyed drug btson la song 'dug rgya mi 'jur ta tshong mkhan zhig la sgor gnyis brgya nyes pa phogs 'dug | nye lam dbyin zla 8 ta rig 14 nyin ka sbug 'ba' rba lags dang rnya rnya 'dzoms pa'i nang nas g.ya' phying [*phyin] sher do dang phyed tsam dang chang 'dzin bzung gi khrims su 'ba' rbar lo 1 btson dang sgor 600 nyes chad | rnya rnya zla 6 btson dang sgor 200 nyes chad khar sgor 215 dngul rkyang gzhung bzhes gnang song | 'on kho pa nas rdo gling khrims dpon chen por skyang du rtsa zhib gnang rgyu'i snyan zhu phul song | dug rdzas 'di'i lag len ma byed chig | Tibet Mirror 8 (6), 7*

[32] For a study of opium policies in the Republic of China, see, among others, Marshall (1976) and Baumler (2007).

[33] The Acts were the following: the Opium Act, 1857 (XIII of 1857); the Opium Act, 1878 (I of 1878); the Sea Customs Act, 1878; and the Dangerous Drugs Act, 1930 (11 of 1930). Legislative functions and executive authority were gradually extended to the provincial governments by means of the constitutional changes of 1911, 1919, and 1935. For more information on the abolition of opium smoking in India, see the first article in *Bulletin of Narcotics* (Cabinet Secretariat 1957).

provincial rules made under the Opium Act, 1878, the manufacture of opium preparations was forbidden, except for individuals who had lawfully purchased the drug for personal use; the limit of opium paste allowed for private consumption was reduced in most of the provinces to one tola (~ 11.66 g) per person (Cabinet Secretariat 1957).[34] In this context, Baba and Nyanya's strong claim of innocence has be understood against the illegal/illicit backdrop that constitutes the conceptual framework upon which borderland flows are presently analysed. As Schendel and Abraham state, "many transnational movements of people, commodities, and ideas are illegal because they defy the norms and rules of formal political authority, but they are quite acceptable, 'licit', in the eyes of participants in these transactions and flows" (1999, 4). For actors engaged in illegal activities, social acceptability ensures that legitimacy "that comes by operating within informal institutional boundaries", which in turn enables them "to exploit opportunities and operate their ventures outside formal institutional boundaries" (Webb, et al. 2009, 493). Opium consumption lacked such widespread social acceptance, not only in China and India, but also in Tibet: when pleading with the Supreme Judge to reconsider their cases, Baba and Nyanya's main concern was not to deny possession of drugs but to distance themselves from any rumours of their own addiction, possibly to safeguard their reputation among fellow Tibetans.[35]

Despite the sensation that similar cases caused in local communities, in the late 1930s the impact of drug trafficking on the illegal economies of the Indo-Tibetan borderlands was negligible. The lack of fundamental factors – social legitimacy, local authorities' connivance, structured inner organisation – essentially compromised the unhindered flow of such a commodity, restricting its circulation to users and petty dealers. Only small quantities of opium paste found their way across the border, usually with travelling Tibetans, mostly from the eastern regions of the plateau, who carried the drug either for personal use or retail sale to co-regionals.

Silent crime: smuggling activities in wartime

Of all the issues printed by Babu Tharchin in the interwar years, only a few are currently available for consultation.[36] Judging from those still extant, it appears that Baba-la and Nyanya's arrest for drug possession in 1936 was the last crime involving Tibetans to be reported in the *Tibet Mirror* up to 1947: regardless of how fragmentary the resulting picture may be, it appears safe to assume that local news was put on hold as global events took over the press. The outbreak of WWII in Europe in 1939

---

[34] The consumption of opium, especially by ingestion, is attested in India since the earliest centuries of the common era (ca. 9th century). Its use as stimulant, sedative, euphoric, and medicine was habitual and pervasive, yet it never became as extensive as in China nor did it engender the same social and political concern; part and parcel of a long standing cultural system that recommended moderate use, opium consumption remained, legally and socially, a venial sin up to the mid-20th century. On the different perceptions of opium in India, China, Britain, and the United States, see Brown (2002).

[35] Regarded as a vice, drug consumption has been object of social condemnation and official repression among Tibetan communities. Although the earliest ban, issued in Bhutan in the 16th century, regarded tobacco, opium was known by Tibetans since the 14th century. It is hardly surprising that in the local imagery, tobacco (*tha mag* or *tha ma kha*) and opium (*tha mag nag po* or *nyal thag*) were related. Over the years, Tibetans came to identify opium (both *madak* and paste) through tobacco lingo: it was the "lie down-tobacco" (*nyal thag*) or the "black tobacco" (*tha mag nag po*), the latter a term suggestive of its evil nature. On the social perception and diffusion of tobacco, cannabis, and opium in the Tibetan cultural world, see Berounsky (2013) and McKay (2014).

[36] The following is a list of issues per volume printed in the interwar years and currently available for consultation at http://www.columbia.edu/cu/lweb/digital/collections/cul/texts/ldpd_6981643_000/index.html (Columbia University Libraries Digital Collections): v. 10, no. 1-4, 6-8, 10-11 (1938-1939); v. 11, no. 1.3, 7 (1942-1943); v. 12, no. 10 (1944); v. 13, no. 1, 9 (1944-1945); v. 14, no. 3, 5-7 (1945-1946). No issues were released in 1941.

soon monopolised the headlines of most newspapers, including Babu Tharchin'. War developments, maps, and interpretations of foreign military and political rationales may have temporarily trumped media coverage of local affairs, yet borderland regions were more active than ever.

In 1941 and 1942, while the world looked with concern at the escalation of the conflict, Indo-Tibetan trade made the agenda of the Government of India, as two issues – namely, the imposition of a limited land customs regime and the introduction of a free transit procedure – were discussed. Both proposals were eventually postponed, the first following the recommendations of Sir Basil Gould, then acting as Political Officer in Sikkim, the second in consideration of the undesirability of unchecked transit of commodities from India to Tibet. Free transit of dutiable goods was at the time granted to a limited number of Tibetan personalities and dignitaries;[37] extending the concession was deemed politically and economically unwise. The issues were shelved, but the matter was far from being cleared.

Addressing the thorny question of export regulation along the Kalimpong route in a demi-official letter to Sir Gould dated June 12, 1943, Hugh Weightman, Joint Secretary to the Government of India in the External Affairs Department, expressed concern over the increase of illegal transit of commodities through Kalimpong. The draft of the missive is hereafter reported in full:

E.A. DEPARTMENT BRANCH   New Delhi
Draft Letter D.C.   Dated: 12-6-1943
No. 5285-X/43   To: Sir Basil Gould, CEG., CIE., P.O. Sikkim

My dear Gould,

I am afraid there has been unconscionable delay in replying to your letter No. 12(16)-P/42 dated 2-11-42 in regard to the regulation of exports to Tibet. This is mainly due to the fact that Commerce Dept. wishes to have the views of Innes [i.e. the Collector of Customs] in Calcutta but he apparently went on leave and was afterwards transferred. Meanwhile of course we had some brief conversation on the subject when you were last in Delhi.

2. The position in regard to exports to Tibet is of course that all goods covered by the G/I [i.e. Government of India] Export Trade Control Notifications require licences before they can be consigned to Tibet unless they are consigned from a foreign country under the transit procedure or unless they are among the comparatively few minor items covered by Open General licence No. 2 of which I enclose a copy. In point of fact, however, the G/I have not enforced their Export Regulations for goods going to Tibet for the simple reason that they have no effective machinery to enable them to do so.

3. Before transit trade to China across Tibet started up, the non-enforcement of these regulations was a matter of little moment since Tibetan imports of goods from India did not impose a serious strain on the supply position in this country and their requirements of goods imported into India were few enough (Chinese brick tea was the main item so long as it came into India by sea). But there is now evidence that valuable imported goods such as watches, fountain pens, jewellery, etc. are being transported from India to China via Tibet and the situation has therefore changed. While the G/I have no desire at all to interfere with the passage across the British Indian frontier of goods meant for normal consumption in Sikkim and Tibet, they are anxious that as far as possible those for China should not be allowed to go out except under cover of an export licence.

4. It is evident enough that a water-tight scheme cannot be operated without interference with normal traffic to Sikkim and Tibet and without the most elaborated system of controls. As I have already said we do not want to interfere with ~~goods meant for consumption in Sikkim and Tibet~~ [deletions in the original; L.G.] Sikkim/Tibet trade and we certainly do not wish to encumber ourselves ~~by setting up~~ with innumerable export control stations along the whole frontier. Thus it becomes a matter of finding a working compromise which goes a reasonable way towards meeting ~~our~~ essential requirements. Thus on the Sadiya-Rima-Likiang route steps have already been taken,

---

[37] The request advanced by the Pangdatsang (sPang mda' tshang) on November 28, 1942 is an example of such practice: the firm, one of the most influential inside and outside Tibet, asked Sir Gould, Political Officer in Sikkim, permission to import to India in instalments 225 bars of silver, for which they had already paid Indian customs duty (National Archives of India, External Affairs, External Brach, Progs. No. 104-X(2)/42, "Import into India of silver bullion and coins, etc. from Tibet", D.O. No. 12(7)-F/42).

in consultation with the Assam Govt., to establish a checking post at Denning, and for exports via Kalimpong it is proposed to instruct the Central Excise staff stationed there to maintain a careful watch on the movement of the following article in particular: -

(i). Piecegoods and yarn, if in large quantities;
(ii). Leather and leather goods;
(iii). Rubber manufactures;
(iv). Synthetic dyestuffs;
(v). Apparel in any appreciable quantities;
(vi). Toilet requisites, especially of the imported kind;
(vii). Paper and stationery (fountain pens in particular);
(viii). Watches;
(ix). Jewellery;
(x). Drugs and medicines; and
(xi). Typewriters.

~~With a view to combating the efforts~~ If attempts are made to export such articles from British India in quantities or of categories which are obviously outside ~~the~~ normal use in Sikkim or Tibet, the Kalimpong Excise staff are being instructed to detain them unless a valid export licence is produced, to refer to the G/I all suspicious items thus detained, to continue to exercise a check on efforts to smuggle currency and jewellery in contravention of restrictions imposed under the Defence of India Rules and to maintain a complete record of the passage of goods of these descriptions with full particulars of their consignors or consignees.

5. It is clearly difficult for the Central Excise officers to discharge their responsibilities with a reasonable modicum of efficiency if they are left without any statistics of the consumption of such articles in Sikkim and Tibet. We should therefore be grateful if you would furnish as complete a list as possible of goods normally imported into Sikkim from British India for local consumption against which goods <u>alleged</u> to be for consumption in Tibet and Sikkim can be checked. Naturally it is realised that such a list cannot be sufficiently exhaustive to cover all possible exports; nevertheless it will serve as a guide to the Customs officials in helping them to decide whether a particular consignment ought to be detained for enquiry although declared as destined for local consumption in Sikkim and Tibet.

It is of course necessary to list any article which is not included in the Export Trade Control Notifications.

Yours sincerely,
Sec. H. Weightman[38]

By June 18, 1943, Weightman's suggestions had been ratified and officially communicated to the Collector of Central Excises and Salt Revenue of North-East India by the Central Board of Revenue.[39] In the early 1940s, transit of dutiable goods across the Indo-Tibetan border acquired new political and economic relevance, due to the heavy demands of wartime efforts on China.[40] Engaged on the eastern front against the Japanese troops since 1937 and increasingly weakened by internal partitions, China struggled to cope. By the latter part of 1940, traditional supply routes had been severed by the Japanese military machine,[41] and the Nationalist government led by Chiang Kai-shek had no choice but to turn to its southern neighbours for support. In 1941, a plan was launched for the construction of a motorable highway connecting Sichuan Province to the NEFA (North-East Frontier Agency) border, in nowadays Arunachal Pradesh. The project, fiercely opposed by the Tibetan government and deemed impractical by the Government of India, was abandoned in favour of an

---

[38] National Archives of India, External Affairs, External Branch, File No. 104-X/42, draft letter by Hugh Weightman to Sir Basil Gould, dated June 12, 1943 (No. 5285-X/43).

[39] National Archives of India, External Affairs, External Branch, File No. 104-X/42, communicate by K. G. Jacob, Second Secretary, Central Board of Revenue, dated June 18, 1943 (C. No. 187-Cus.II/43).

[40] For an in-depth study of the almost forgotten role played by China in WWII, see Mitter (2013).

[41] By 1941, Japan had complete command of the sea and control over the railways in the lower part of the Yangtze Valley, thus forcing the KMT government to relocate to the westernmost provinces of Sichuan and Yunnan.

alternative route through Burma. The highway, the construction of which started in December 1942, linked the Assam rail and river head at Sadiya and Ledo to Lungling in Yunnan Province via the Mong-Yu junction of the old Burma Road,[42] thus bypassing Tibet completely (Goldstein 1989, 378-381).[43]

Regardless of British attempts to both sustain China's resistance and alleviate Tibetan apprehensions of territorial encroachment, the Indo-Tibetan route via Kalimpong remained the easiest and fastest way through which goods could be moved. In July 1942, five months before work on the Ledo Road began, Frank Ludlow, the head of the Lhasa Mission, was instructed to exert pressure on the Tibetan government to impress on them the seriousness of the matter. In London and New Delhi, rumours of China's imminent fall were met with extreme anxiety – it became imperative to ensure a swift transit of supplies through Tibet. Threatened with economic restrictions and political backlash, the Tibetan government agreed to allow transport of non-military goods for a year, to be conducted through Tibetan trading companies and along established trails and arranged centres. The issue seemed resolved, yet only a month later, the Chinese Ministry of Communication requested the right to hold direct negotiations with Tibetan transport firms in Kalimpong, a demand that was met with strong hostility by the Lhasa government.[44] The ensuing trade embargo imposed by the latter ended in April 1943, amidst threats of military repercussion by the Chinese; the removal of the ban was presented by the Tibetans as a concession to the British in honour of the friendship ties between their countries and no Chinese was allowed to accompany the goods without permission (Goldstein 1989, 385-389).

In a demi-official letter to Weightman dated August 20, 1943, Sir Gould expressed his position in the matter of exports to and via Tibet in a point by point manner, advocating once again the institution of a free transit procedure to Tibet and strongly opposing the grant of export permits to individual traders. In his view,

> [...] picking and choosing between individual exporters will be highly insidious, and will amount, from the point of view of the recipients in China, to the establishment of a black market, right away as far back as Kalimpong. Temptations to the officials concerned would be very great. If it is decided there must be a system of permits for the export of only limited quantities, or certain classes of goods, it may be necessary to grant the quota to some Chinese authority. But it will be far better to avoid restrictions of quantities of specific goods, or of the total of goods, and not to invite official Chinese interference.[45]

Sir Gould's concern over a black market of permits *ad personam* – and his hinting at corruption and bribery of local officials – was not without foundation. In the early 1940s, Chinese interests in Kalimpong increased substantially, as did the involvement of Tibetans in the trade, both legal and

---

[42] The Burma Road was the first line of supply used in wartime, as it connected Lashio in Burma (nowadays Myanmar) to Kunming in China. Supplies were shipped to Rangoon (today Yangon) in Burma and transported via railway to Lashio, where they were loaded on trucks. Work on the construction of the motorable road started in 1937 and were concluded in 1938. The Burma Road was eventually overrun by the Japanese in 1942. For more information, see Webster (2003).

[43] Originally known as Ledo Road, the highway was renamed Stilwell Road in 1945, in honour of the American general Joseph Stilwell, who directed its construction. On the complexities of the China-India-Burma theatre during WWII and the role played by the United States, see Webster (2003).

[44] "Mr. Wong Pong, representative of the Chinese Ministry of Communications, has been in Kalimpong attempting to negotiate with Tibetan traders whose reply so far has been as anticipated, namely that they are only prepared to deal with him if ordered to do so by the Tibetan government. Mr. Wong Pong informed the Assistant to the Political Officer in Sikkim that he intended to report to Chungking his failure to achieve results." National Archives of India, External Affairs, Far Eastern Branch, File No. 683(3)-FE/44, express letter (secret) by the Governor General (External Affairs Department) to Secretary of State for India, London, dated January 4, 1943 (No. 7/S).

[45] National Archives of India, External Affairs, External Branch, File No. 104-X/42, demi-official letter by Sir Basil Gould to Hugh Weightman, dated August 20, 1943 (D.O. No. 12(2)-P/43).

illegal, across the border. Although no news of local criminal activities was reported in the *Tibet Mirror* for most of the 1940s, an illegal border economy was thriving and its social actors' meddling transcended any national or ethnic divisions – crime was, in many ways, a catalyst for globalisation.

In criticising the "ethnic" conception of crime, recent scholarship has forcibly argued for an alternative view that prioritises social networks and situational context rather than ethnicity (e.g. Soudijn and Kleemans 2009; Kleemans and van de Bunt 2009). Transnational activities (e.g. smuggling) add new dimensions to the relationship between ethnicity and crime, because offenders benefit from contacts between different nations and different ethnic groups. In the trans-Himalayan borderlands, profit-driven traders and merchants of India, China, Tibet, and Nepal cut market niches in the cross-border trade for themselves, smoothly threading in and out of the legal framework.

When the Tibetan embargo on the transport of supplies to China fell in 1943, many Chinese firms hurried to take advantage of the Lhasa-Kalimpong route: high demand faced consignment limits and permit restrictions though, and smuggling occurred at an increasingly higher frequency. Often, illegal and legal practices overlapped, as undeclared goods were despatched as part of authorised consignments, customs officials were bribed or coerced into acquiescence, or commodities were sold without permits. Such market-based crimes represent an important facet of illegal economies: high level of demand for particular goods (e.g. food grains, cotton, arms) or services (e.g. prostitution, smuggling) combined with high profit and low penalty risks provide "ideal conditions for illicit business groups to enter the market to seek profits by organizing the supply" (Lodhi and Vaz 1980, 145, as quoted in Helfgott 2008, 271).

On August 26, just a few days after his demi-letter to Weightman, the Collector of the Excises and Salt of North-Eastern India Rai Bahadur Shiv Charan Das addressed the Secretary of the Central Board of Revenue regarding the control of exports to China via Kalimpong. The first points raised by the Collector are hereafter reported in their entirety in light of their relevance to the topic at hand:

DEPARTMENT OF CENTRAL EXCISES AND SALT, NORTH EASTERN INDIA
C.No. 11-Et/43/17745 dated Calcutta, the 26th August 1943

From   Rai Bahadur Shiv Charan Das, B.A., A.M.I.B.E. (Eng.),
            Collector,
            CENTRAL EXCISES AND SALT, NORTH EASTERN INDIA,
            Calcutta
To   The Secretary,
            Central Board of Revenue,
            Simla
Subject:- Foreign Trade Control – Exports to China via Kalimpong
            Prevention of without license -.

Sir,

   I have the honour to refer to the Board's letter C.No. 187-Cus, II/43, dated the 16th June 1943.

2.   This Department is receiving from time to time intercepts of trade messages between China and India forwarded by the Censor, and acting on the information in these intercepts consignments intended for China, notably medicines and piece-goods and other articles indicated in your letter referred to above have been detained by the staff of this Department at Kalimpong. The fact that no license is required for the export of goods for bona fide consumption in Sikkim and Tibet has gradually become known to trade interests both in Kalimpong and elsewhere; and it is being taken undue advantage of, for it has been noticed that exporters now invariably give Tibet as the intended destination of their goods when challenged. A reference is here invited to Mr. N.R. Pillai's letter No. C-I11014-CWA/42, dated the 1st August 1942 to the Collector of Customs Calcutta (copy of correspondence enclosed for ready reference). In consultation with the then Collector of Customs and Foreign Trade Controller, Mr.

F. M. Innes, the policy followed hitherto has been to detain all large consignments connected with persons whose names had appeared in the Censor's intercepts.

3. In connection with the tightening of control on the Kalimpong border the following points deserve consideration: -

    (a). Appreciable quantities of raw wool are carried by mule transport into India by Tibetan merchants. It has been urged both by trade interests and the Political Officer, Sikkim, that there should be no interference with the carriage back to Tibet by such mule transport of simple merchandise such as salt, kerosene oil, sugar, brick tea, tobacco, wearing apparel, cotton piece-goods, yarn etc. for bona fide consumption in Sikkim-Tibet. Actually, however, it has been found that the same muleteers are often employed also for India-China trade via Tibet, and once a whole transport train has got ready it is impossible to tell in the absence of any dependable statistics of the past trade with Tibet how much is intended for carriage to China, especially when the muleteers assert with readiness for violence that all the goods are for Tibet.

    (b). There is no Land Custom station at Kalimpong and it is not possible to check the content of every package intended for transport across the Indian frontier. This Department's officers who are empowered under Section 6 of the Sea Customs Act proceed under Section 171 of the Act on suspicion, such suspicion being generally aroused when, as indicated above, the traders or muleteers concerned are noticed to have figured in the Censor's intercepts. There are of course other sources of information as well.

    (c). There are, as already indicated above, no accurate statistics of the quantity of variety of goods which have in the past been going across the border for bona fide consumption in Sikkim and Tibet. My staff has locally compiled some statistics which show that trade ostensibly with Tibet has nearly doubled itself during the last three years. The increase may or may not be due merely to a genuine increase in demand and confirms the suspicion that a part of the goods declared for use in Tibet is filtering through to China.

    (d). The Censor's intercepts frequently take a long time reaching my Department. In any case, it is not possible without the help and co-operation of the Political Officer, Sikkim and the British Trade Agents in Tibet or the Tibetan authorities to stop goods at Kalimpong when it is stated by the transporters that they are meant for consumption in Sikkim-Tibet though some of these must ultimately go to China.

    (e). Confidential intelligence collected from informers seems to indicate that there is perhaps some influential Tibetan behind the import of unlicensed goods to China. [*handwritten addition*] [...][46]

From the above, it is clear that Charan Das' aim was to impress the need for additional officers at the Customs station of Kalimpong, as agents were needed to inspect packages and patrol the routes from Pedong and Rangpo to the border. His missive also reveals much of the sensitivity of borderland regions to international and supranational events: transnational flows, triggered by China's demand for supply, overrun the stricture of the law, spilling over into grey zones regulated by illegal micro-practices.[47]

---

[46] National Archives of India, External Affairs, External Branch, File No. 104-X/42, "Foreign Trade Control – Exports to China via Kalimpong. Prevention of without license", missive by the Collector of Central Excises and Salt, North-Eastern India to the Secretary of the Central Board of Revenue, dated August 26, 1943 (C.No. 11-Et/43/17745).

[47] In a confidential letter to N. R. Pillai, Additional Secretary of the Commerce Dept. dated July 14, 1942, the Collector of Customs F. M. Innes laments that "there has [...] been a good deal of smuggling [...] from Dum Dum and Dinjan. [...] Our efforts to check this were handicapped by several circumstances, mainly because Chinese officials and quasi-officials shamelessly abused the privileges and courtesies which they were accorded." (National Archives of India, External Affairs, External Branch, File No. 104-X/42, copy of Confidential D.O. letter C.No. 135(War)/40).

In wartime, communications between Chinese traders operating in Kalimpong and buyers in mainland China were systematically intercepted by British India censorship, as increased control over the air route from Dum Dum or Dinjan diverted Chinese interests towards the land trails passing through Sikkim. Merchants became more and more skilful in avoiding the censors' net, often resorting to cryptic wire messages or hand-delivered letters. On December 4, 1943, a telegram attracted the attention of a surveillance operator.[48] The note, dispatched by a certain Wangyunbao in Likiang (today's Lijiang in Yunnan Province) to a Chokochung in Kalimpong, read as follows: "TSHUISHIHTA SAFETY LIKIANG BRING LETTER RECEIVE ALL". The intercept was forwarded to the Central Intelligence Bureau for further investigation, and on June 2, 1944 a final report was submitted to the External Affairs Dept. for information:

> "Nothing definite could be found out as to the real sense of the telegram which CHOKOCHUNG received from WANGYUNBAO, Lekiang [*sic*]. It may however be noted that CHOKOCHUNG is a Chinese trader very much interested in the smuggling of illegal goods to China via Tibet.
> The 'letter' referred to in the telegram is probably one dealing with the purchase or sale of certain illegal goods, which the sender does not wish the Government to know about, as they are certainly very much aware of the fact that letters are censored nowadays.
> This is not the first time that the question of smuggling of letters arises. Many incidents have been reported especially from Tibet to India and vice versa.
> Any further light on this subject will be dispatched immediately."[49]

In the early 1940s, Chinese interests in Kalimpong increased substantially, as did the involvement of Tibetans in the trade, both legal and illegal, across the border. The complexity of the local socio-economic fabric forced newcomers to tread carefully and gauge their chances against competitors. Insights on the matter may be gathered by a letter intercepted by the Indian censorship in May 1944: the message, a report sent by an employee of the Pekin Syndicate in Calcutta – a certain N. T. Ivanoff – to the firm's branch in London, regarded the possibility of a caravan route to China via Kalimpong. The missive was flagged by the censor as indicative of smuggling plans. An excerpt is presented here, as it contains information on the situation on the ground.

KALIMPONG

> In reference with instructions contained in your letter of the 17th instant, I proceeded to Kalimpong on that date with a view of ascertaining the existing conditions and facilities in connection with despatches to, storage in, and despatches from Kalimpong by caravan route to China of various cargoes – mostly Cotton Yarn and cloth.
> As a result of my observations and investigations I compiled a detailed Report – enclosed herewith – which can be briefly summarised as under: -
>
> 1. TRANS-SHIPMENT OF CARGO FROM MAIN RAILWAYS TO KALIMPONG can be arranged without much difficulty.
> 2. Very satisfactory <u>GO DOWNS</u> can be secured at Kalimpong with aggregate space of 25,000 sq. ft. – sufficient to accommodate 6,000 bales of Yarn and/or Cloth.
> 3. Satisfactory arrangements for <u>REPACKING</u> can be made with one of the Contractors in Kalimpong.

---

[48] The diffusion and commercialisation of modern technologies such as the telegraphy brought a new level of connectivity, virtually crossing any physical border. Yet, fast and apparently unhindered communication came with a price, especially for those active on the illegal front. The susceptibility of telegraphic communications to interception meant an increased risk of content disclosure (Sen 2021, 417), which in turn translated into several arrests among smugglers, dealers, and spies. Regarding the Chinese reliance on the British telegram service since its installation across the Indo-Tibetan border in the aftermath of the Younghusband Expedition, see Zhang (2021).

[49] National Archives of India, External Affairs, War Branch, Progs. Nos. 42(39)-W/44 (Secret), "Censorship Interceptions --- Telegram from Wangyunbao, Lekiang to Chokochung, Kalimpong regarding smuggling of illegal goods to China via Tibet".

4. ORGANISING THE CARAVANS is best done through Contractors. In view of many difficulties connected with this task, we should avoid accepting responsibility for despatches from Kalimpong, confining our undertaking to delivery of goods to Kalimpong, storing them there, and if necessary, repacking.
5. PACK-ANIMAL TRANSPORT TO CHINA takes from six to eight months for the cargo to reach its destination.
6. CUSTOMS FORMALITIES must be arranged with the Customs Authorities in Calcutta.

*   *   *

"Chinese colony in Kalimpong: The original Chinese colony in Kalimpong, of about seventy, has swelled to over 400 during the past two years. […] The majority of the newcomers are engaged in transport businesses between India and Tibet and China. I have been informed that smuggling is going on here on a very great scale, and is mostly organised by Chinese.

Demand for pack animals is great, and competition in bids for the mules is very acute, and would develop into open hostility between the various firms were it not for innate Chinese oberance and co-operation when abroad. Reasons for the competition is shortage of mules, and any newcomer planning to engage in shipping goods either to Tibet or China is regarded as a most unwelcome and undesirable addition to the existing community. My impression is that even senior members of staff of certain respectable Chinese firms in Kalimpong are carrying on, as a side line, transport business, probably on their own. This is the only way I can explain their reluctance in giving detailed information in respect of technicalities of despatches. […][50]

Further glimpses of the merging of Chinese and Tibetan interests – and their impact on the border illegal economy – are contained in a point by point report on Chinese activities at Kalimpong drafted by the Director of Intelligence Bureau (D.I.B) and dated October 2, 1944. The D.I.B.'s note provides additional information on the matter of illegal transport across the border, especially regarding the local balance of powers:

[…] Several Chinese and Tibetans including local Merchants from Kalimpong are carrying on illicit trade via Tibet on a large scale. One Woods Ding (TING WU SHIH 11253, 12744, 9982) was granted an Export license for 200 bales of cotton by the Government of India, but was compelled to return the consignment to Calcutta for want of mule transport.

It is also reported that owing to conditions ruling at present, it is not possible to prevent this illicit trade which is reported to be carried on openly via Tibet. […][51]

Mule transport to and from Kalimpong had been traditionally dominated by Tibetans and Newars, a situation that had remained substantially unaltered up to the mid-20th century (Harris 2008, 207).[52] Limited availability of pack animals and groups' monopoly on the transport business on one hand and restrictive export policies on the other strengthened the incidence of smuggling and black market across the border, an event that did not fail to attract the attention of the Government of India.

In late September 1944, a secret report was dispatched to the External Affairs Dept. by Capt. Albert R. Allen on the matter of smuggling through Kalimpong.

SECRET. SECURITY PROBLEMS. Report on a trip made by Capt. A. R. Allen to Kalimpong from the evening of 22nd Sept. to noon of 27th Sept. 1944

---

[50] National Archives of India, External Affairs, Central Asia, Progs., Nos. 504-CA/44, "Report on the Chinese at Kalimpong", dated June 2, 1944.

[51] National Archives of India, External Affairs, Central Asia, Progs., Nos. 504-CA/44, "A note on the Activities of the Chinese at Kalimpong, District Darjeeling", dated October 2, 1944.

[52] The effect that demand had on transport rates is well exemplified by the following consideration by N. T. Ivanoff, the employee of the Peking Syndicate, Ltd.: "[i]t would be advisable to exercise as such secrecy as possible in respect to the volume of our shipments - large consignments invariably reflect on the rates on mules […]." National Archives of India, External Affairs, Central Asia, Progs., Nos. 504-CA/44, "A note on the Activities of the Chinese at Kalimpong, District Darjeeling", dated October 2, 1944.

Kalimpong's security problem is closely linked up with Sino-Tibetan commercial activities. For a correct understanding of the former it is essential to know something of the latter, though this will be dealt with in full by the Commercial Attaché, Calcutta.

THE CHINESE COMMUNITY. There is a population of 300 Chinese according to registrations with the Darjeeling Police, but this cannot be taken as an accurate figure for the following reasons:

1. A large number are traders who travel frequently.
2. There are transients, who stay for an average of 15 days, just long enough to repack their goods in Kalimpong and arrange for Tibetans to transport them to Pharijong and on to China, who do not report their arrival to the Police.

Sub-Inspector Kalu Singh Rai, Alien Registration Section Kalimpong, estimates these transients at about 100, most of them Yunnanese.

In the town itself there is only one Chinese restaurant, one or two small Chinese shops, a Chinese school and a bank. The rest of the Chinese are merchants engaged in the Indo-Tibet-China overland trade. Their main business being cotton yarn and piece goods.

This trade is at the present in the hands of 9 Chinese firms. [...]

Their method of operating appears to be, buy the cotton yarn and piece goods from Marwaris in Kalimpong then get Tibetans to take it over in their godown for repacking and transportation to China via Tibet. The Chinese therefore do not actually handle or transport the goods, nor do they use their names on the packages.

EXISTING SECURITY MEASURES. In March 1943, a Deputy Superintendent of Excise was posted to Kalimpong. Although his duties were heavy, he was given no Land Custom's powers for export and was not given the right of search. In cases where, in his opinion, a search was necessary, permission had to be obtained from the Deputy Commissioner through the Sub-Divisional Officer.

In May 1944 an understanding was reached between the External Affair Department and the Central Board of Revenue whereby exports to Tibet were restricted to a figure of 10 tons daily. Under the new scheme the Deputy Controller of Excise ceased to function in connection with the control of export trade and the scheme was administered by the Political Officer, Tibet, Sikkim, and Bhutan. The Political Officer's staff were to check the daily quantity of exports by counting mule loads crossing the Jelep La and Natu La, 12000 feet above sea level. As from the beginning of Sept. the Bengal Cotton Cloth & Yarn Order, 1944, forbids the export of any cotton cloth or yarn whatsoever, whether intended for China, Tibet or elsewhere.

From this it may be seen that the Chinese could pick any article or document with their cotton yarn or piecegoods and nobody would have been any wiser. 12000 feet above sea level in mid-winter is hardly the place to conduct a search of pack loads. Security control was very weak indeed. [marginalia: *It* [i.e. search] *is not conducted at the passes but at Gangtok and Rangli.* (signature unintelligible)].

With the present ban on the exports of cotton cloth and yarn, it should be a much simpler job to check goods etc. passing the various frontier police out-posts, but from evidence obtained it appears that the police guards are not as secure as they should be.

It was reported that recently about 20 mule loads of cotton cloth (40 maunds [~ 1,493 kg]) had been smuggled out of Kalimpong to Tibet via Pedong. At Pedong the Police Constable stopped the muleteers and, it is alleged, received a bribe of Rs. 3 per bale (Rs. 120/ - in all) and allowed the goods to pass through. On the day of Capt. Allen's trip down to the Police Out-post at Rishi Bridge, 4 miles beyond Pedong, he counted 2 horse loads and 17 porter loads of cloth being carried by Tibetans. It was evident that the police at Pedong had allowed them to pass. The Police Out-post at Rishi Bridge consists of two unarmed Nepali policemen, which is inadequate for the task of preventing Tibetan traders armed with knives from getting their goods over the border. It may also be noted that there is no telephone connection between Kalimpong, Pedong and Rishi Bridge.

INDIA-TIBET COMMUNICATION. The foregoing has been concerned with the two regular routes into Tibet from Kalimpong.

1. Kalimpong-Pedong-Jelep La-Yatung.
2. Kalimpong- Rangpo-Gangtok-Natu La- Yatung.

If however the ban on the export of goods is not lifted soon, it is most probable that other routes will be used, e.g.

1. From Sukhia Pokhri to Western Nepal, the Tibetan frontier and on to China.
2. From Kathmandu, Nepal, to the Tibetan frontier.

There are longer and harder routes but if traders are desperate to get rid of their goods, the difficulties of these routes would not be considered insuperable. These other routes are:

1. Via the Almora Hills
2. Via Gharwal

3. Via Pesharsh Estate (Simla) to Gartok, Gyanima, Chakra to Western Tibet
4. Via Kashmir to Ladakh

It may be seen therefore, that a complete check on personnel and goods leaving India for Tibet and China by overland routes is well-nigh impossible.

CHINESE AGENTS.

It is believed that there are two centres which may be the headquarters of Chinese agents.

1. The Home Studio, this is operated by a Chinese, Champa Yosel, who is commonly called Se Kushoe by the Tibetans.[53] He is known to be very interested in the present position of the British School in Lhasa, and contacts his Tibetan friends in the hope of obtaining information about it. It is improbable that he could support himself in the style in which he lives if he were dependent upon the business he does.

2. 'Morningside'. This is one of the three well-furnished bungalows occupied by Chinese from Yunnan, most of whom come from Tengchung [i.e. Tengchong]. The leader of the group is a man called YIN Pen-tsung (13270/8846/11976) who was a staff member of the Yunnan Mule Route Transportation Administration, Kunming, but who is known to have declared that he is not at present doing anything in the way of business. A close watch on the activities of this man might produce a good dividend, but this is not so easy when he does not use the post office for forwarding his mail.

Capt. Allen had the opportunity of spending an evening in the company of the members of this group. During the conversation it was learned that all of them intended to return with their families to their native homes, as soon as the road was clear. They hoped that the India-China Road would be open by Chinese New Year (February), which might suggest that their attentions were to be transferred to the new road. One of the Chinese said he intended to buy a couple of trucks here in India which he would hire out to the Chinese Government for the transportation of military supplies. They were aware of the fact that the road was to be under military control and only to be used for military supplies, yet one cannot but be suspicious of the possibility of carrying on private business under the guise of carrying military supplies. During the evening a friendly tone was maintained by the group, and an invitation was given to the officer to meet them again next day. It appeared however, that owing to his connection with the Police, their suspicions were aroused in the meantime, and the second evening spent with them was marked by a much less friendly atmosphere. Mr. Yin seemed to be anxious to get the officer to talk, and ordered a whole bottle of whisky for him in the hope of gaining his purpose. The Police in Kalimpong and one or two Tibetans strongly suspect that he is an agent, though nothing definite was discovered during the officer's stay there.

THE BANK OF CHINA – KALIMPONG. […] It is considered by some that the activities of the Bank's staff as possible participants in the smuggling trade would repay investigation. The extent to which the Bank itself is involved in the financing of this trade is not known, for the officials in the Bank preserve considerable discretion about their activities. […]

THE FUTURE IMPORTANCE OF KALIMPONG. It is the opinion of some that the importance of Kalimpong will lessen when the new India-China Road is opened, but with the building of several motor roads in West China extending to the border of Tibet, and with the granting of telegraph facilities to Chinese merchants in Lhasa, this is very doubtful. Messages may be carried by traders as far as Lhasa, then speeded on their way to China. It would appear that China is going ahead with her plans to win over the people of Western Tibet, and Kalimpong presents a unique centre for such activity, having wealthy Tibetan merchants residing or represented there.

---

[53] The case of Champa Yosel cautions against an uncritical acceptance of state-imposed ethnic categorisations. The arbitrary identification of local agents as alternativelty "Chinese", "Tibetans", or "Indians" could be, and often was, "strategically harnessed in service of a range of political agendas" (Sen 2021, 414). Champa Yosel is the misspelling of the Tibetan name Jampa Özer (Byams pa 'od zer), while the appellative "Se Kushoe" is clearly a rendition of Tibetan term "Se Kushok" (Tib. *se sku gzhogs*) or, more frequently, "Se Kushab" (Tib. *se sku zhabs*), a honorific form used to address the sons of Central Tibetan aristocrats. His name, although spelled differently (i.e. Jampa Wosel) also figures in KMT documents, where he is listed as an informant for the Chinese government. The British intelligence records however present a different picture. In a note dated December 10, 1946, Champa Yosel/Jampa Wosel is reported being a KMT informer and collaborator of the famous Pangdatsang Rapga (sPang mda' tshang Rab dga), a Khampa revolutionary and scion of one of the wealthiest trading firms of Tibet (McGranahan 2005, 2017; Sen 2021, 429). Champa Yosel/Jampa Wosel's activities in India ended on December 31, 1946, following his arrest and the issuance of an "Order of Deportation" (Sen 2021, 430). On state-imposed ethnic categorisations and their function in terms of border security and intelligence in 20th-century Kalimpong, see, in particular, Sen (2021).

There is the other problem of Chinese entering India in Tibetan dress, and thus dispensing with the need to register as aliens. This may assume greater importance as the Western Tibetans become more friendly towards them, and will demand the presence of a Chinese speaking officer at Kalimpong to keep check on new arrivals. At present there is no person there who speaks or reads one word of Chinese, and this is serious as it is the main back door into China. With the existing staff and their very limited powers, it will be impossible to tighten up security. There must be someone on the spot to interrogate people in Chinese, and able to read any Chinese script produced from packages or personal belongings. To rely on Calcutta for any urgent help in these matters is at the present out of the question, for Capt. Allen sent an urgent telegram to Calcutta asking permission to extend his stay in order to follow up certain openings; but the reply came five days later, after he had reluctantly left for his unit. Such time delays would be avoided if there was someone there able to make decisions.[54]

The interlacing of Tibetan and Chinese interests was a matter of concern for the Government of India and its frontier cadre.[55] On December 20, 1944, Hugh E. Richardson, at the time serving as Joint Secretary of the External Affairs Dept., forwarded to the Major G. Sherriff, Head of the British Mission in Lhasa, a photograph, with a key, of a gathering held in Kalimpong in June of the same year. The photograph portrayed more than thirty people, both Chinese and Tibetans.[56] Sherriff could only confirm and offer some insights on the identities of sixteen of them; twelve participants remained therefore unknown.[57]

Though troubled by the looming of China over Tibet, His Majesty's Government advised caution, a recommendation shared by the India Office, the Government of India headquarters in the capital of the Empire, already in mid-1943. There was a general understanding in London that the withdrawal of British recognition of Chinese suzerainty claims would precipitate the events in Tibet, leading to a military incorporation of the plateau. Such a blunt about-turn would also compromise Britain's standing in the war – at the time, China was the only Allied power opposing Japan in the Far East (Goldstein 1989, 397-400).[58] London's directives may have been clear but did not prevent the frontier cadre from keeping a watchful eye on Chinese movements in Lhasa and Kalimpong, since His Majesty's Government's refusal to commit to openly supporting Tibet vis-à-vis China "greatly increased the pressure on the Tibetan government to yield to the pro-Chinese elements in Tibet and seek a bilateral agreement with China" (Goldstein 1989, 419).

Political uncertainties, war demands, and trade restrictions created in Kalimpong a climate ripe with economic possibilities, of which admittedly few were legal. Met with fierce competition, newcomers had to ease themselves into a complex social fabric; creating connections with locals was therefore essential, especially if they planned to escape law strictures. As stated above, mule transport

---

[54] National Archives of India, External Affairs, Central Asia, Progs., Nos. 557-CA/44 (Secret), "Report on a trip made by Captain A.R. Allen to Kalimpong in connection with Kalimpong security problems and Sino-Tibetan commercial activities".

[55] For an in-depth study of British India-Tibet relationship in the early 20th century and the role played by the frontier cadre in it, see McKay (1997).

[56] The frontier cadre was especially concerned by the activities of Shen Tsung-lien, who replaced the controversial and little-loved Dr. H. H. Kung as Chinese liaison officer in Lhasa in late 1943. Shen surrounded himself with educated, often English-speaking individuals and his Buddhist faith and understanding of local culture won him the approval of the conservative sectors of Tibetan society. Shen's appointment was part of Chiang Kai-shek's attempt to regain the friendship of Tibet after the relationship between the two countries plummeted in 1942-1943. See Goldstein (1989) and Smith (1996).

[57] National Archives of India, External Affairs, Central Asia, Progs., Nos. 504-CA/44, demi-official letter by H.E. Richardson, Joint Secretary of the External Affair Dept. to G. Sherriff, Head of the British Mission in Lhasa, dated December 20, 1944 (D.O. No. D.3211-CA/44) and demi-official reply dated January 26, 1945 (D.O. No. 3(3)-L-45).

[58] For a more exhaustive comment of the India Office's position, see FO371/35755, Tibet and the question of Chinese suzerainty, dated 10 April 1943, quoted in Goldstein (1989, 399-400).

along the Lhasa-Kalimpong route was mainly controlled by Tibetans: they took charge of the packed goods and despatched them under their firms' names. As reported by Capt. Allen, it was not unusual for muleteers to turn into illegal carriers.

Although lacking the organisational maturity, hierarchical structure, diversification, and multi-jurisdictional capacity of criminal groups, Tibetan smugglers presented a few features ascribable to organised crime consortia, such as rent-seeking, member loyalty, and the pursuing of government officials' corruption (Whitaker 2002, 133). They also did not refrain from the use of violence when challenged: possession of arms was widespread among Tibetan floaters/transients and represented an additional cause of concern for the local police. Knives and swords were part of the traditional attire of nomadic groups from Eastern Tibet, and it was normal practice for muleteers to carry a weapon, be it cold steel or firearm, for personal protection against thieves and robbers. Although socially "licit" within Tibetan circles, the custom of weapon bearing had been outlawed in India since the late 19th century, when the passage into law of the India Arms Act, 1878 prohibited manufacture, conversion, sale, import, export, transport, bearing or possession of arms, ammunition or military stores to non-authorised individuals,[59] and prescribed as penalty for breach of rule an imprisonment extendable to three years, or a fine, or both. The India Arms Act, 1878 supplemented Section 326 in Chapter XVI (of Offence Affecting the Human Body) of the Indian Penal Code (IPC), which had come into force in 1862. In 1946, five Eastern Tibetans were arrested by the Kalimpong police for weapon possession and condemned in accordance with Section 326 of IPC.[60] As reported in the *Tibet Mirror*,

> On October 6, 1946, Döndrup (Don grub), a native of Amdo Zangpo [i.e. an area in Amdo, Eastern Tibet] residing at Tenth Mile in Kalimpong, and the Khampas Tashi Püntsok (bKra shis phun tshogs), Wangdü (dBang 'dus), Jampa Tsering (Byams pa tshe ring), and Wangdrak (dBang grags) were arrested by the police for possession of a knife in accordance with Section 326 of the Indian Penal Code, and on February 1, 1947 the tribunal condemned each man to two years of prison.[61]

As previously clarified, the issues of the *Tibet Mirror* preserved in the Columbia University's collection offer us only a scattered and fragmentary picture of the interwar years, especially in relation to local crimes and Tibetan involvement in them. Starting from the early months of 1947, the number of issues available for consultation increases substantially, the latter a fact that supports a more balanced reconstruction of the actual news coverage of local events.

---

[59] "No person shall go armed with any arms except under a licence and to the extent and in the manner permitted thereby. Any person so going armed without a licence or in contravention of its provisions may be disarmed by any Magistrate, police-officer or other person empowered by the President of the Union in this behalf by name or by virtue of his office. For the purpose of this section, 'arms' includes also knives with pointed blades rigidly affixed, or capable of being rigidly affixed, to the handle, and measuring in all over five inches in length, which are intended exclusively for domestic, agricultural or industrial purposes. [...]" Section IV, point 13, India Arms Act, 1878.

[60] "Voluntarily causing grievous hurt by dangerous weapons or means – Whoever [...] voluntarily causes grievous hurt by means of any instrument for shooting, stabbing or cutting, or any instrument which, used as a weapon of offence, is likely to cause death, or by means of fire or any heated substance, or by means of any poison or any corrosive substance, or by means of any explosive substance, or by means of any substance which it is deleterious to the human body to inhale, to swallow, or to receive into the blood, or by means of any animal, shall be punished with [imprisonment for life (subs. by Act 26 of 1955, s.117 and the Sch., for 'transportation for life')], or with imprisonment of either description for a term which may extend to ten years, and shall also be liable to fine." Section 326, Indian Penal Code.

[61] *snga lo dbyin zla 10 tshes 6 nyin gyi mtshan la ka sbug me li bcu par sdod pa don 'grub zhes par a mdo bzang po ba dang | bkra shis phun tshogs | dbang 'dus | byams pa tshe ring | dbang grags khams pa rnams nas gri'i lag len byas 'dug pa rnams la rgya gar khrims yig ang grangs 326 nang gsal ltar pu li sis 'dzin bzungs gyis nye lam dbyin zla 2 tshes 1 nyin khrims khang nas mi rer lo gnyis re'i btson la btang 'dug | Tibet Mirror* 15 (4-5), 4.

Growing pains: Indian commodities control polices in the aftermath of Independence

The 1945-1947 period saw changes at a global and national level. The Allies had won the war, but victory came at a hefty price: heavy investments of labour force into war productions, destruction of most of the European industrial infrastructure, and loss of millions of lives drastically altered the status quo ante bellum, in Europe as in Asia.

In 1945, the general election marked an unprecedent reversal of Conservative parliamentary representation in Great Britain, with the issue of granting independence to India becoming the main order in the political agenda of His Majesty's Government in the post-war immediacy.[62] While Labour and Tories fiercely debated over the transfer of power and its procedures,[63] the political and social situation in the subcontinent was rapidly deteriorating.

By the start of 1947, the republican-minded Congress seemed increasingly inclined towards full-on independence, and tensions with the Muslim League spilled out in the streets, translating into civil unrest and protests.[64] The unworkability of a Congress-League coalition and the incapacity of the government to confront communal riots compelled common acceptability of a most drastic solution: the surgical partition of Punjab and Bengal (Sarkar 1989, 436; Owen 2003, 427).[65] On the midnight of August 14-15, 1947, while the formula freedom-with-Partition went through the motions, the new regimes' birth pains turned into death throes along their dividing borders: the new dominions of Pakistan and India came to life bathed in blood.[66]

In the twenty-nine months from Independence Day (August 15, 1947) to the establishment of the Republic of India (January 26, 1950),[67] the country was ruled by an interim government headed by

---

[62] The prelude to post-war negotiations was set in the last months of the conflict, with sporadic British efforts to conjure a joint participation of Congress and Muslim League in the existing structure of the central government (Sarkar 1989, 414).

[63] Hoping to stir India towards the status of Dominion in the Commonwealth, the Tories demanded that the transfer of power be unhurried, orderly, and honourable, labelling the Labour's decision to hand over executive power to a Congress-dominated interim government with no prior agreed-upon constitution-making procedure "a blunder of the first order" (note dated December 13, 1946 as quoted in Owen [2003, 411]). After months of negotiation with Indian leaders on the issues of the interim government and the principles and procedures to follow in the drafting of a new constitution for independent India, in May 1946, the Cabinet Mission came out with a plan that temporary appeased both Congress and League, although the agreement proved short-lived. Eventually, after months of pleading and threatening by the Viceroy, a Congress-led interim government headed by Nehru was sworn in on September 2, 1946 (Sarkar 1989, 428-432). By that date, Lord Wavell had already suggested in the final draft of his "break-down plan" a total withdrawal of British forces by March 31, 1946 (Sarkar 1989, 447).

[64] Common riots of unprecedented scale had broken out in India since mid-August 1946: starting from West Bengal (Calcutta) in August, touching Maharashtra (Bombay) in September, spreading to East Bengal (Noakhali) in early October, Bihar in mid-October, Uttar Pradesh (Garhmukteshwar) in November, to engulf the Punjab from March 1947 onwards (Sarkar 1989, 432).

[65] Known as the "Mountbatten Plan", from the incumbent Viceroy of India Louis Mountbatten, the idea of partitioning the country into two separate dominions had been gaining consensus among the British government long before his assignment to India. Mountbatten's merit, if any, was to expedite the process, thus leading to a series of anomalies that affected the actual arrangement of the Partition (Sarkar 1989, 447-450).

[66] Pakistan was a federation of five provinces: East Bengal (nowadays Bangladesh), West Punjab, Balochistan, Sindh, and the North-West Frontier Province (NWFP), later joined by the Punjab princely states (Bahawalpur, Khaipur, Swat, Dir, Hunza, Chitral, Makran, and the Khanate of Kalat), see Talbot (1998). By August 15, 1947 all Indian states, except Kashmir, Junagadh, and Hyderabad, had been incorporated into the new dominion of India, thus relinquishing control over defence, external affairs, and communications to the central government of the Union (Sarkar 1989, 451). For a comparative analysis of both the mechanisms of boundary drawing and the social consequence of Partition, see, among others, Talbot and Singh (1999). On the retributive character of genocide in the Punjab in 1946-1947, see Brass (2003).

[67] The Constitution of India, drafted by a committee headed by the jurist Bhimrao Ramji Ambedkar and accepted by the Constituency Assembly on November 26, 1949, came into effect on January 20, 1950, thus making of India a democratic republic.

the Prime Minister Jawaharlal Nehru. In the aftermath of the Partition, immediate actions were taken towards the containment of severe inflationary pressure and shortages of primary sources. To this end, proactive economic policies were adopted to incentive the industrial sector, and key industries were temporary nationalised. Control over essential commodities, introduced as an anti-hoarding measure in wartime and progressively relaxed in 1946, was tightened again in 1947, as explained in the *Indian Information*,[68] issue dated February 1, 1947:

> The case for continuance of controls even after the war emergency is over rests on the fact that inflation is still unabated and there is an acute shortage of goods in the country. […] India is not in a fortunate position to increase the supply of goods all at once […] Nor India is able to increase supplies by imports as there are not enough surpluses abroad. (102)

The ultimate operating authority in regard to most of these controls were the various Provincial Governments, with the Central Government playing an advisory role, on the basis of the suggestions advanced by an independent Commodity Price Board.[69] To regulate the export of various commodities, among which figured prominently essential supplies – such as foodstuffs, textiles, coal, and iron – a licence system was introduced in May 1947, and quotas assigned for those countries to which such exports were allowed. In spite of the post-war global market's high demands, the institution of export permits restricted the international flow of commodities through legal channels, thus increasing the payoffs for those willing to disregard any regulatory strictures. Although the porosity of the Indo-Tibetan border allowed for alternative routes, making virtually impossible the application of a water-tight scheme of border control, a substantial amount of illegal transit still occurred through the regular route via Rangpo-Gangtok-Nathu La pass. Due to meteorological instability and geomorphological fragility though, the latter was considered the least favourable among the official passes leading to Kalimpong through Sikkim; it is not surprising therefore that some tried their odds against the customs officials.

Despite the incidence of the phenomenon, illegal trade across the Indo-Tibetan border was, for all intents and purposes, petty smuggling carried out by single individuals or small groups of people with vested interests in the matter. Such networks, lacking any structural organisation, mostly relied on ethnic affiliation or personal connections, as demonstrated by the following articles published in the joint issue 4-5 of the *Tibet Mirror* dated February-March 1947.

> Since on December 13, three Tibetans – the trader Tsering, *co* [= *ajo*, i.e. term of respect for man] Tsering, and Wangdü – transported to Tibet 21 *mon do* [~ 784 kg] of local rice, [according to what is] clearly [stated] in Section 18 of the Penal Code,[70] the Kalimpong police office arrested them in Rongpu [i.e. Rangpo] on the border of Sikkim, and on February 18, they were sentenced to pay about 300 rupees each, in addition to the immediate confiscation of the local rice.

---

[68] Edited by A. S. Iyengar, Principal Information Officer, *Indian Information* aimed to provide a condensed record of the main activities of the Government of India.

[69] Set up in March 1947 for a period of three years, the Commodity Prices Board had the task (i) to advise, in the light of all relevant data, what prices, or price limits, either the Central Government or a Provincial Government should fix for commodities; and (ii) to keep under constant review the movements of commodity prices in India, suggesting, when necessary, whether the price of any commodity not controlled should be controlled and, if so, what price, or price limits, should be fixed for that commodity (*Indian Information* 20 (203), 227, dated March 1, 1947).

[70] At the time of the events reported in the *Tibet Mirror* (early 1947), Sikkim was a princely state in a subsidiary alliance with the British Raj, and although not directly ruled by India, it followed its penal code. Section 18 of the Indian Penal Code (IPC) regards the territorial jurisdiction of India, where the term "India" means, accordingly to the Interpretation Act, 1889, "British India together with any territories of any native prince or chief under the suzerainty of His Majesty exercised through the Governor-General of India, or through any governor or other officer subordinate to the Governor-General of India" (52 & 53 Vict. c. 63, s. 18).

On December 19, at Rongpu on the Sikkimese border, the police arrested a muleteer who was transporting 25.5 *sher* [~ 24 kg] of white sugar. He was sentenced on January 18 to pay about 100 rupees.[71]

Textile confiscated by the Kalimpong police office → On February 1, the local police office, after searching the shop of an Indian named Kalyan Baldev Das, confiscated 30 loads (*do po*) [~ 1,120 kg] of the Kalimpong Textile Syndicate and quite a lot of cloth both boxed and not boxed in crates, as well as two crates of textile that had been carried to the transport station of the iron ropeway known as "Kalimpong-Girling" and [other] two crates of cloths ready to be sent to the same Girling. Now, it is rumoured that the local police confiscated 12 crates of textile on the borders close to the ropeway, Siliguri, the local district of the Kishanganj – a region of Bihar (India), and the Gorkha (i.e. Nepalese) area of Jyagbani ('Jag ban) [in Bihair]. The news has come that Kalyan [of] Kalimpong has been arrested. Furthermore, it is reported that two Tibetan men, who said to be the assistants of the Indian trader Kalyan, had also been arrested, since six loads [~ 224 kg] of textile were despatched from their houses. In addition, it is reported that, due to the confiscation, a Tibetan trader called Tsültrim (Tshul khrims), who had left at Kalyan's 22 loads [~821 kg] of textile, was taken into custody. Yet it is rumoured that, since the trader Tsültrim did not have a permit but rather bought the 22 loads of textile from three false Tibetan traders, he was kept in custody for a few days and then released on bail.[72]

Interethnic collaborations played a relevant role in the context of border illegal economies: the existence of shared interests between diverse groups triggered the formation of criminal comradeships that operated in the margins of legality. In the increasingly cosmopolitan Kalimpong, multi-ethnic links criss-crossed local society, aiding the circulation – legal and illegal – of bodies and commodities alike. Authorised shops owned by Indian retailers supplied a legitimate front for the black market of licensed commodities, thus providing Tibetan and Chinese traders with a means to exceed any earmarked export quotas, while Tibetan muleteers or Newar contractors were recruited for cross-border transport, often eased by bribes to complicit government officers stationed at checkpoints.

In spite of their ramifications and broad scope, such criminal networks lacked the hierarchical organisation and internal stratification of mafia-like crime syndicates and remained rather basic and small-scale. In the eye of the Government of India, the amount of goods smuggled via Kalimpong patently did not justify the costs of setting up a hard border, although the old issue of establishing a land customs line against Tibet recurred again soon after the end of the war, when reports on the matter were requested from both the Political Officer in Sikkim and the Collector of Central Excises in Calcutta. With the future constitutional position of Sikkim still uncertain, the Ministry of Finance (Revenue

---

[71] *kha sngon dbyin zla bcu gnyis pa'i tshes 13 nyin* → *bod tshong tshe ring dang | co tshe ring | dbang 'dus bcas mi gsum nas yul 'bras mon do 21 bod du 'don 'dren byed par khrims yig ang grangs 18 nang gsal ka sbug pu li si'i las khung nas 'bras ljongs sa mtshams rong pur 'dzin bzungs thog nye lam dbyin zla 2 tshes 18 nyin khrims khang nas yul 'bras gzhung bzhes thog mi rer sgor mo 300 tham pa re nyes pa btang 'dug pa'i gnas tshul || dbyin zla 12 tshes 19 nyin rong pu sa mtshams su pu li si nas drel pa zhig gis bye ma kar sher phyed nyer lnga khyer nas 'gro bar 'dzin bzung gis khrims khang nas dbyin zla 1 tshes 18 nyin bye kar gzhung bzhes thog dbyin sgor 100 tham pa nyes pa btang 'dus || Tibet Mirror* 15 (4-5), 4.

[72] *ka sbug pu li si'i las khungs nas ras cha 'dzin bzung* → *nye lam dbyin zla 2 tshes 1 nyin 'di ga'i pu li si'i las khungs nas rgya gar kan ya sbal bde ba dāse zhes pa'i tshong khang brngogs nas ka sbug sin ṭi kaṭ kyi ras cha do po 30 tsam dang | ras cha sgam du blugs pa dang ma blug pa mang tsam dang | ka sbug sgir ling zhes pa lcags thag tu do po 'or 'dren sa tshigs su khyer 'gro ba'i ras sgam 2 dang | sgir ling rang du gtong chog chog ras sgam 2 bcas 'dzin bzung byas shing da dung go thos su 'di ga'i pu li si nas shi li gu ri dang | rgya gar sbi har khul gyi sa gnas ki shagin khul | 'jag ban zhes pa gor yul dang thag nye ba'i sa mtshams nas ras cha do po 12 'dzin bzung byas gshis | ka sbug kan yar 'dzin bzung byas pa'i gnas tshul || yang rgya tshong kan ya'i g.yog po yin zhes bod mi 2 kyi nang nas ras cha do po 6 'thon stabs de dag kyang 'dzin bzung byas skad | yang bod tshong tshul khrims zhes pa zhig nas ras cha do po 22 kan ya zhig gi nang du bzhag par 'dzin bzung gis do dam gnang ba'i gnas tshul || yang go thos su tshong tshul khrims nas ras cha do po 22 de rnams bod tshong brdzus ma gsum gyi rtsa nas nyos pa las kho rang la par mi ṭi lag 'khyer med skad | kho rang la nyin shas do dam gnang rung khag theg 'gan len thog lhod yang byung 'dug pa'i gnas tshul || Tibet Mirror* 15 (4-5), 4.

Division) vetted the proposals under consideration (i.e. the imposition of a limited land customs regime along the Indo-Tibetan border and the introduction of a free transit procedure for goods to Tibet) and rejected them. The reasons given were the same provided in 1941 and 1942, when the twin questions of a customs line against Tibet and free transit procedure to that country were first advanced. The decision, taken by the Revenue Division in late October 1947 and ratified by the Ministry of External Affairs and Commonwealth Relations two months later, was forward for information to Arthur John Hopkinson, then acting as Political Officer in Sikkim. In a demi-official letter to Vallillaih Madhathil Madhavan Nair, Under Secretary to the Government of India, Ministry of External Affairs and Commonwealth Relations, dated January 28, 1948, Hopkinson doubts the feasibility of turning the enumeration posts at Gangtok and Rongli into weighing stations for statistical purposes:

> […] 3. I do not think it worth while going to the length of insisting on weighment by means of scales at these way-side posts. This would entail great inconvenience to the caravans of miles which would have to off load and re-load, and before long we would have to have a pretty strong force to enforce it: whereas it can be safely assumed that each load on either side of a mule is approximately one maund [~ 37 kg], the usual standard.
> 4. Nor can you, on the present standards, expect a searching examination of a large percentage of the actual loads, for this too, by the nature of the case, would involve very grave inconvenience, the opening of carefully packed bales by the way side, possibly in the rains, breaking of nailed boxes and soforth, and this would also lead to a riot before long if insisted upon. In the case of ordinary loads, there is no reason why muleteers should lie about their contents, and any how an experienced person can pretty well tell by the look and the feel of the package (e.g. whether it is tea, cloth, cigarettes and soforth, which has its distinctive appearance and feel).
> 5. Should, however, there be any deliberate intention to smuggle either way small articles of great value (e.g. precious stones, gold and so forth) it will be in practice beyond the power of Enumeration posts to detect this; nor was this the object with which the post was set up at the start as correspondence shows. Such an object can only be realised by the method of customs intelligence. But I do not think that this is of practical interest at the moment; even if precious stones are going up or down it does not much signify at present. […][73]

Despite the Political Officer's confident assertion, smuggling of valuables from Tibet proved to be substantial, to the extent of affecting the economies of the borderland regions. Starting from 1948, an increasing number of Tibetans, either permanent residents or transients, were arrested and charged for illegal import of Chinese silver coins under Section 8 ("Restrictions on import and export of certain currency and bullion") of the Foreign Exchange Regulation Act, 1947.[74] Since the Act's inception in March 1947, customs officials along the Indo-Tibetan border tightened their control over the route to and from Kalimpong, yet throughout 1948 the amount of silver, ingots, and coins trickling in from China via Tibet swelled into an underground river, threatening to burst the border open. The situation worsened significantly in the following years, when the rise of the Chinese Communist Party (CCP) led by Mao Zedong generated a ripple effect that swept through the whole of Southeast and Central Asia. The Republic of India, still taking its first, uncertain steps in the dawn of Independence, witnessed with concern the establishment of the People's Republic of China on October 1, 1949 and the subsequent

---

[73] National Archives of India, External Affairs, North East Frontier Branch, File Progs., Nos. 16(3)-NEF/48, demi-official letter dated January 28, 1948 from the Political Officer, Sikkim to Ministry of External Affairs and Commonwealth Relations (D.O. No. 12(2)-P/46).

[74] "The Central Government may, by notification in the Official Gazette, order that, subject to such exemptions, if any, as may be contained in the notification, no person shall, except with the general or special permission of the Reserve Bank and on payment of the fee, if any, prescribed bring or send into India any gold or silver or any currency notes or bank notes or coin whether Indian or foreign" (Foreign Exchange Regulation Act, 1947, section 8, point 1).

encroachment of Communist forces on Tibet: the northeast border has suddenly become an extremely sensitive one.[75]

A silver flow: petty smuggling in the late 1940s and early 1950s

The economic implications that the CCP's policies had on the Himalayan borderlands in general, and on Kalimpong in particular, have to be understood against the broad historical backdrop of post-war Sino-Indian relations and the role played by Tibet in them. Whilst Britain and India were going through the painful motions of decolonisation, China was facing a harrowing civil war. After an eight-year (1937-1945) period of ceasefire, during which all efforts were directed towards Japan, the hostilities that had intermittently opposed Nationalist and Communist factions since 1927 resumed in earnest. The CCP eventually gained the upper hand, yet victory was far from complete: the political and economic systems were in turmoil, pockets of Nationalist resistance were still active in areas of southwestern China, and to complicate matters further the ethnic minority provinces of Tibet, Xinjiang, and Inner Mongolia were not under control (Weatherley 2006, 15). As early as July 1949, the acting head of the Chinese Mission in Lhasa had been summoned in front of the Tibetan Cabinet of Ministers and accused of harbouring Communist agents among his staff. In the light of the charges, all Kuomintang officials, including members of the hospital, school, and wireless station were ordered to return to China forthwith. The ousting of Chinese personnel marked a dramatic shift in Sino-Tibetan relations: for the first time since 1913-1914, China had no officials stationed in Tibet. The day the People's Republic was formally established, Tibet stood de facto independent (Goldstein 1989, 613-614).[76]

Given the incompleteness of the CCP's hegemony over the whole PRC, administrative control was initially divided among six regional bodies (northwest, north, northeast, east, southwest, central south), of which only the north and northeast were CCP's strongholds. In the other four regions, the administrative power had to be temporarily ceded to the party's military wing, the People's Liberation Army (PLA) (Weatherley 2006, 16). Concerned that the CCP's reunification policies might impugn Tibet's right to self-rule, the Cabinet of Ministers invested in military modernisation, while despatching diplomatic missions to the United States, Great Britain, Nepal, and India, despite the fact that relationships with the latter had been strained since 1946.[77]

Tibet's opening towards the global stage had already started in mid-1947, when rumours of an impending victory of the Communists had stung its government into action. Amidst a currency crisis that threatened to unbalance the country's economy, and eager to gain international visibility, the Cabinet of Ministers had approved the setting up of a Trade Mission in the summer of 1947. Officially charged with the immediate securement of hard currency reserves from India, the mission had the

---

[75] On the Sino-Indian frontier and the role of Tibet in Sino-Indian relations in post-colonial times, see, among others, Gupta (1974) and Norbu (1997).

[76] In the secreted annual report on the Indian Mission, Lhasa, dated 1949, the Tibetan government's decision, "taken with surprising secrecy and firmness", is reconducted to three factors: (1) prevention of any Communist infiltration through the office of the Chinese Representative; (2) public assertion of Tibet's independent status, before CCP could claim sovereignty over it after the collapse of the Nationalist government; and (3) retaliatory action to the insult caused by the KMT's installation of the 10th Panchen Lama at Kumbum (sKum 'bum) Monastery in June 1949 (National Archives of India, External Affairs, R&I, File No. 3(17)-R&I/50, Memorandum No. 3(13)-L/50).

[77] In the post-war immediacy (1945-1947), Indo-Tibetan relationships had suffered a diplomatic setback. Old tensions over the McMahon Line in the Tawang area and British reluctance to actively support Tibet's demands for self-government fuelled a Sino-Tibetan rapprochement, which led to the unfortunate participation of Tibetan representatives at the National Assembly of 1946 in Nanking and the consequent inclusion of the country into the Chinese constitution (Goldstein 1989, 550-559).

additional task of ensuring the direct purchase of gold from the United States.[78] When the representatives of the Tibet Trade Mission arrived in New Delhi in November 1947, their reticence to acknowledge the Republic of India as the legitimate successor of the British Raj in the geo-political arena of Southeast Asia was answered by Nehru with a flat refusal to release any substantial amount of foreign currency.

In the course of 1948, the Tibet Trade Mission visited China, the United States, and Great Britain, with few to no results in economic or political terms. Despite treating the members of the mission with great courtesy, neither of the two Western powers committed themselves to the Tibetan cause; the Nationalist front proved even less satisfactory, as Chiang Kai-shek firmly upheld his understanding of Tibet as part of China. The Trade Mission nevertheless obtained a small victory: in January 1949, negotiations resumed with the Indian government regarding the release of hard currency for the purchase of gold, the non-conversion into rupees of the foreign exchange gained through Tibetan exports, and the establishment of a free-transit procedure for goods imported to Tibet via Indian ports. Out of these requests, India agreed only to the release of $250,000 for the procurement of American gold bullion (Goldstein 1989, 579-606).[79]

In his history of modern Tibet, Goldstein unexpectedly ascribes the Indo-Tibetan deadlock of 1947 to relatively minor diplomatica and financial issues. Apparently, India resented Tibet's territorial claims and the request of reimbursement from previous exports, whereas the Cabinet of Ministers begrudged Nehru's lack of financial and diplomatic support (Goldstein 1989, 575). Such an interpretation cautions against an uncritical reliance on interested witnesses: Goldstein's understanding of the matter was in fact largely based on private conversations held with Richardson in May 1984. The latter's reading of the situation, although plausible, lacks depth. India's reluctance to cede part of its hard currency to Tibet must be framed, I argue, within a wider context of economic stagnation, recurrent inflationary spirals, and speculative and hoarding practices that characterised the country since the end of WWII.

Between 1945 and 1947, the war-time system of price control of consumption goods, supplemented by partial rationing of food grains, sugar, and textiles, was maintained, with side supply channels accommodating additional demand at black market prices. In November 1947, prompted by a temporary standstill of the inflation, the government embarked upon a programme of progressive reduction of rationing and price control of essential supplies. The removal of protective measures caused an immediate rise in the prices of food grain, sugar, and textiles, which gained in intensity in the following months, to the extent that the government was forced to reintroduce controls and price ceilings in July 1948 (World Economic Report 1948, 42-43). Market sensitivity to the Reserve Bank of India's containment of deficit financing through injections of new notes determined an inflation of credit; the easy expansion of money contributed to the rise of prices, in India as in China, where the situation reached unique proportions.[80]

---

[78] Tibet did not have access to hard currency (U.S. dollars or pounds sterling): any foreign payments were deposited into the Reserve Bank of India and there credited into rupees to Tibet's account. The conversion from hard to soft currency decreased Tibet's profit and forced the country into a position of dependency on its southern neighbour (Goldstein 1989, 571-572).

[79] According to a series of telegrams between the U.S. State Department, the U.S. Secretary of State, and the U.S. Embassy in India dated May 1949, the Tibet Trade Mission bought gold bullion for a total of $425,800. The purchase was made through the Hong Kong-Shanghai Banking Corporation. The extra $175,000 apparently came from private funds as well as repayment of old loans granted by the Tibetan mint to traders (Goldstein 1989, 606, fn. 124).

[80] For a more general overview of the financial situation in Asia and the Far East in 1946-1947, see Economic Report 1945-1947 (1948, 86-89).

Here, steady rises of prices and short "spending periods" continued to reinforce each other throughout 1947 and a good part of 1948. In August of that year, a monetary reform was launched by the KMT in an attempt to curb the hyperinflationary process: to secure hard backing to the new note, the gold yuan, the government requested all holdings of silver, gold, and foreign currency to be yielded to the central banks and converted to gold yuan at a fixed exchange rate.[81] After a short interval of relative stability, old habits resumed and none of the subsequent measures introduced by the Nationalist government were successful in halting the inflationary spiral (World Economic Report 1948, 43-44). Uncontrollable devaluation caused a rapid fall of the gold yuan value: all incomes were immediately spent in consumption, as paychecks were rushed to market before they lost their purchasing power. Those who could invested heavily in gold and silver, although the demand for foreign currency remained relatively low due to slow production recovery in exporting countries and transport bottlenecks (Economic Survey of Asia and the Far East 1947, 187).

The rush to safe-haven assets reintroduced into the market old silver coins that had been demonetised following China's abandonment of the Silver Standard in 1935. Issued at a nominal value of 10c, 20c, 50c, and one yuan dollar, these coins – most of which dated from the first decade (1915-1928) of the Republic of China (ROC) – presented considerable variations in terms of silver content, due to a high incidence of debased specimens.[82] Despite being prohibited by the CCP, private possession of silver – be it in the form of coins or bullion – continued to be a socially licit practice, providing a hidden pool from which silver yuan dollars trickled into the local economy, thus contributing to the general hyperinflation. The silver coins that circulated in the markets of the westernmost provinces of China seeped through the cracks of the law and eventually spilled into the margins of legality. As side drains flanking traditional trade routes, informal channels syphoned silver from the markets of Yunnan and Sichuan Provinces to the urban centres of Eastern and Central Tibet and from there to the Himalayan trade hubs.

Due to global inflationary trends and national restrictive policies, neither silver nor gold could be imported to or exported from India without a Reserve Bank permit – the latter a measure that the absence of a land customs line made it impossible to implement in any effective way. Small quantities of Chinese silver were constantly smuggled by Tibetan muleteers and traders to Kalimpong, where they entered the local economy as payoffs for illegal transactions. Throughout 1948, news of arrests and confiscations were reported by Babu Tharchin on an almost monthly basis;[83] tellingly, most of those involved as local dealers and fences were of Tibetan origin.

Much like any other flow dynamics, economic flows tend towards homeostasis: in other words, when two or more economic systems interact, any disequilibria between them translate into fluctuations

---

[81] Between 1939 and 1947, hyperinflation and a series of devaluations determined the creation of three different exchange rates that run simultaneously. Of these, two were official (one for limited transactions and another, considerably higher, for all other authorised transactions) and one illegal. The latter was significantly lower than the level justifiable by demand and supply of foreign exchange (Economic Survey of Asia and the Far East 1947, 186). Tellingly, the exchange rate was one gold yuan for three million old Chinese dollars (法幣 *fabi*) or four gold yuan per American dollar, the same rate (twelve million *fabi* per U.S. dollar) applied in the black market at the time of the reform (World Economic Report 1948, 44).

[82] Regardless of the existence of precise standards of fineness set at 900, Chinese mints progressively reduced the content of silver to enhance the margins of profit in the minting process. Before demonetisation in 1935, the standard of the yuan dollar was at 880 fine, but in case of smaller denomination, such as complementary 10c and 20c coins, the standard could be as low as 400 fine. On the debasement of the Republican silver coins in general, and in Yunnan Province in particular, see Wright (1992).

[83] Reports of silver confiscations and arrests of smugglers appear in the six issues of *Tibet Mirror* dated 1948, four of which belonging to volume 16 (January, February, June, and July 1948) and two to volume 17 (October and December 1948).

converging to a set point of balance. In conditions of equilibrium, demand and supply naturally compensate each other, and their interaction determines the price at which a certain commodity is sold (equilibrium price). In a basic economic analysis, an artificial state of equilibrium – in which all factors affecting the quantity of a demanded commodity (e.g. market variations, changes in income and consumers' preferences, seasonal effects) are held constant – makes it possible to plot the fluctuations in price of that commodity on a downward-sloping curve, known as the demand curve: the lower the price, the higher the consumers' willingness to buy. Similarly, in the same artificial state of equilibrium – in which all factors affecting the quantity of a supplied commodity (e.g. price of substitute products, production rates, availability and cost of labour) are held constant – fluctuations in that commodity's prices may be plotted on an upward-sloping curve, known as the supply curve: the higher the price, the more willing the producers will be to sell. In an open market, the price mechanism regulates demand and supply towards the equilibrium price; the same basic rationale is at the core of import demand and export supply. When protectionist policies are implemented though, total restrictions or partial interruptions of flows affect the economic homeostasis, thus unbalancing the systems of all the countries involved. The increase in silver smuggling in 1948 was the symptom of a deep-seated and widespread supranational economic distress. Paradoxically, the same legal idiosyncrasies that crippled licit Indo-Tibetan border trade ended up fuelling the illegal sectors, creating grey niches of bureaucratic ambiguity. Although aware that the import and export of silver and gold were strictly regulated, the lack of certainties regarding the issuing of permits and the loose meshes of the border control net provided enough reasons to question the legitimacy of police interventions, as the following excerpt from the *Tibet Mirror* issue dated January 1948 illustrates:

> Confiscation of Chinese silver → It is said that there is a lawsuit following the confiscation on November 5 of Chinese silver adding up to a weight of [the value of] more than 1,200 rupee[84] from the house of the Tibetan trader Lobsang Künga (Blo bzang kun dga') by either the office of the Kalimpong police or the on-site police officer in charge, Mr. Andru Tsering (A 'brug tshe ring). Although there are strict orders prohibiting the export of Chinese silver or white silver from Tibet, white silver arrives in great quantity, thus it is not known whether permission to import [silver] had been requested from the government.[85]

In the attempt to solve some of the uncertainties connected to the import and export of silver, gold, and legal tender, a Tibetan translation of the relevant bulletin issued by the Ministry of Finance was made available to the readers of the newspaper in June 1948, fifteen months after the implementation of the law:

> 12th (11th) Bulletin from the Indian Finance Office, March 25, 1947: As written in FI/47: without carrying a permit of the bank known as "Reserve Bank" no trader is allowed to import on Indian soil or export from India: (a) gold *tam*, gold sheets, gold dust, gold leaves, not beaten molten gold; and (b) silver *tam*, bricks of Chinese silver, silver bits, silver leaves, silver dust, silver sheets, types of unfabricated silver items and currencies that do not circulate in the banks of one's own country. According to Section 7 of last year (1947)'s legal act [i.e. Foreign Exchange Regulation Act, 1947], whoever is without the permit of the bank known as "Reserve Bank" is not allowed to import or

---

[84] Although the Tibetan text reads *dbyin sgor*, a term generally used to indicate British currency (sterling pounds), in this context its reading as "rupees" appears more likely. Indian rupees are usually rendered in Tibetan as *hin sgor*, but the relatively new independence of India could have justified the use of *dbyin* either as a near-homophone for *hin* or as a slight anachronism for the [British]-Indian rupee. I am grateful to Charles Ramble for clarifying the difficult interpretation of the term for me (private conversation, June 2017).

[85] *rgya dngul 'dzin bzung* → *ka sbug pu li si'i las khungs sam sa gnas gyi pu li si'i do dam pa sku zhabs a 'brug tshe ring mchog nas bod tshong blo bzang kun dga'i sa nas dbyin zla 11 tshe 5 nyin rgya dngul dbyin sgor 1200 tsam gyi ljid byas pa 'dzin bzung gnas nas kha mchu yod pa'i gnas tshul || bod nas rgya dngul lam dngul dkar phyi 'khyer mi chog pa'i bka' rgya btsan po yod kyang dngul dkar ni mang po 'byor kyi 'dug | de 'ang gzhung sa mchog nas 'khyer chog pa'i dgongs pa zhus min cha ma rtogs || Tibet Mirror 16 (3), 3.*

export valuables [such as] gold, silver, types of [precious] stones and so on when crossing the Indian borders: this must be borne in mind by the Tibetan traders – large, medium, and small.[86]

Regardless of Babu Tharchin's efforts to educate his fellow countrymen, confiscations of silver continued throughout the following months; even well-known Tibetan firms, which were in the habit of renting out part of their facilities to external traders to be used as depots, were partially affected by the toughening of policing control.[87]

In the issue of the *Tibet Mirror* dated August 1948, the publisher tackles head-on the thorny matter of the trade barrier, adding his personal understanding of the situation. The editorial is presented here in full:

> Opinion on the silver trade: India and Tibet proclaimed that exporting silver is not allowed without obtaining permission from one's own government, yet silver worth about 10,000,000 rupees arrives in Kalimpong from Tibet to India every year. After selling this silver out, Indian commodities are imported to Tibet. If they block the influx of silver, the trade between India and Tibet will not be good. Why? How it would be possible to buy and export the goods by blocking the capital funds of trade? Nowadays, all the global countries have amicable relationships by trading with each other. They even wage war through trading. We wonder if it would not be good – if the harmonious relationship between India and Tibet also were to rely on trade – if the two governments considered, by discussing [the matter] with one another for it not turn into a mutual loss, whether it will be possible to export and sell silver. The Indian Government is really not to be blamed at all: for instance, if one converted the cost value of the abovementioned quantity of silver to tola, [which is] the weight of a coin per single mould (*ko ro*), there would be silver for about 6,500,000 tola; if one calculates a customs duty of 4 anna per tola, the government would get about 1,600,000 rupees. If one thinks about that, the Indian Government cannot be blamed [for blocking the import of silver]. Anyway, if, after talking with each other, the customs duties were decreased, or if there was a way of relaxing [them], we wonder if that will not establish the roots of harmonious relations between the two countries and stop the traders' suffering. Furthermore, if silverwares are brought to the country from abroad, would it not be beneficial for the country itself? Yet, as for the reasons of blocking the import of silverwares, [would it be better] not to do so, lest it turns into a great loss to the country through customs duties? Again, [that is] our opinion. We wonder: would it not be possible to import for sale the Tibetan *sang* and the *tamkar* with a 10-denomination [or], for example, the silver *tam* that are allowed to circulate in one's own country? [Or] to distribute all the silver items, such as pieces of Tibetan silver, by casting [them] in a 3 *sang tamkar* [i.e. all Tibetan silver should be cast into a coin of 3 *sang* denomination]? The exports would greatly benefit the commoners of the country, but only if there was no dilly-dallying [on the matter]. If I made the mistake of writing my very humble opinion, please bear with me. It is said that these days a *sang* gets 1 rupee and 10 anna.[88]

---

[86] *rgya gar dngul rtsis khang gi las khungs nas 'das lo 1947 dbyin zla 3 ta rig 25 nyin spel ba'i rtsa tshig ang 12 (11) – FI/47 par 'khod gsal : – re dzarb sbeng zhes pa'i dngul khang gi bka' 'dzin lag 'khyer med par : – (ka) gser ṭam | gser leb gcug [*gcig] | gser phye | gser shog | gser zhun rgyab min dang | (kha) dngul ṭam | rgya dngul sa phag | dngul hrob | dngul shog | dngul phya [*phye] | dngul leb | dngul chas ma bzos pa'i rigs dang rgyal khab so so'i dngul khang du 'gro rgyugs mi byed pa'i sgor mo bcas tshong pa su zhig nas rgya gar sa steng du tshur 'khyer ba'am rgya gar nas phar 'don nam yang byed mi chog | 'das lo 1947 pa'i khrims lugs ang grangs 7 pa nang gsal ri dzab sbeng zhes pa'i dngul khang gi lag 'dzin med par su zhig nas kyang rin chen gser dngul rdo rigs sogs rgya gar sa mtshams brgal nas 'don 'dren mi chog ces pa'i gsar 'gyur 'di la bod tshong che 'bring chung gsum nas thugs zhib yod pa 'tshal || Tibet Mirror* 16 (9), 8.

[87] In the issue dated July 1948, silver belonging to a Tibetan man was confiscated from the facilities of the Pangdatsang firm: "Another confiscation of 15 loads [~ 560 kg] of silver: on June 24, from the go-down belonging to the Pomda (sPom mda', i.e. Pangdatsang) caskets of silver (weighing) 15 loads have been confiscated. The owner, said to be Tsa Trülbu (Tsha sprul bu), departed for Tibet on the 23rd" (*yang dngul do po bco lnga 'dzin bzung | dbyin zla 6 tshes 24 nyin ka sbug spom mda'i khang khongs sgo dam zhig nas dngul sgam do bco lnga 'dzin bzung byas 'dug | bdag po tsha sprul bu yin skad ta rig 23 nyin khong rang bod la thon pa'i gnas tshul thos || Tibet Mirror* 16 (10), 5).

[88] *dngul tshong skor bsam 'char | rgya gar dang bod gzhung gnyis kas rang rang so so'i gzhung gi bka'i gnang ba ma thob par dngul phyir gtong mi chog pa'i bka' khyab yod 'dug kyang | bod nas rgya gar du lo re'i nang ha lam dbyin sor 10000000 tsam gyi dngul ka sbug tu 'byor gyi yod tshod 'dug | dngul 'di phyir btsong nas*

In arguing for a loosening of the import ban and the implementation of customs duties, Babu Tharchin touches upon the dangerous interactions between illegal sectors and the legal economy: the growth in local demand following the restrictions imposed by the Government of India created the perfect environment for informal institutions to thrive. In the pursuit of profit, authorised Tibetan traders bypassed the strictures of the law and financed legal transactions with illegally imported silver, procured for them either by disenfranchised dealers, such as transient smugglers, or well-connected local fences. Babu Tharchin's call for customs duties to ease the import of silver within a legal framework brings to fore the contradictions between border as seen by state ideology and border as praxis. It is at the border, as van Schendel and Abraham put it, that "the state criminalizes certain forms of mobility but clashes with other state practices condoning or encouraging such border crossings" (2005, 24).

The trade barriers imposed on imports of silver from Tibet or China (via Tibet) did not discourage the local market: on the contrary, the high profit margins determined by the rising demand made the operations of non-organised informal institutions profitable enough to offset the risks involved. Unwilling to bear the costs of a land customs line – necessary if they were to implement import duties – the Government of India resorted to an enforcement of local surveillance through the dispatchment of a few additional police officers to Kalimpong, yet no effective measures were implemented to dampen domestic demand for silver items. As Peter Andreas aptly says in reference to the U.S.-Mexican divide, border policing may, in such cases, take on the features of a "ritualized spectator sport" (2001, x): a series of ineffectual policies broadcast to the national audience as example of state control.

As a result, confiscations of silver continued throughout the last months of 1948, with occasional frictions that threatened to turn into the sort of diplomatic issues against which Hopkinson had cautioned the government.

> News from Kalimpong. Chinese silver → On October 1947, the Lhasa-based Tsarong (Tsha rong) household sent a petition to the Indian government through the Officer in Sikkim to ask for a pass that allowed the import from Tibet to India of Chinese silver, yet, before the pass was issued, Tsarong's workers in Phari, most probably being certain that the pass had been issued, sent 10 loads [~ 373 kg] of Chinese silver to India. Because of that, the representative of the Customs Duties Office of the Indian Government and the police stopped [the goods] saying that it was not allowed to import [silver] without a pass. In the meantime, the Indian Government emitted permits allowing the transport in India of 100 loads [~ 3,730 kg] of Chinese silver, and on November 25 the House of Law of Kalimpong returned the abovementioned 10 loads [~ 373 kg] without legal punishment

---

rgya zog bod du 'dren gyi yod tshod 'dug | gal srid dngul 'byor rigs 'dzin bzung bkag thabs gnang na rgya gar dang bod gnyis kyi dbar tshong lam yag po yong tshod mi 'dug | gang la zer na tshong gi ma rtsa bkag pas tshong zog nyo 'dren ji ltar thub kyi red | deng 'dzam gling rgyal khab tshang ma phan tshun tshong gi thog mthun lam byung ba red | tshong thog nas dmag 'thab kyang byung ba red | rgya bod gnyis kyi mthun lam kyang tshong la rags lus na phan tshun gnyis la sku gyong mi chags pa'i ched du gzhung phan tshun bka' mol thog dngul rigs 'don tshong chog pa'i dgongs bzhes gnang na mi legs sam | ma gzhi rgya gar gzhung la thugs khag gtan nas mi 'dug cing | dper na gong gsal dngul 'bor ma gnas ko rol gcig la sgor mo'i ljid to lar phab na to la 6500000 tham pa tsam gyi dngul yod 'dug par to la rer sgo khral a na 4 re rtsis na gzhung la dbyin sgor 1600000 tham pa tsam babs kyi yod 'dug | 'di la bsam na rgya gar gzhung la thugs khag med tshod | gang ltar gzhung phan tshun gnyis nas bka' mol gnang nas sgo khral skyon thabs yang na lhod yang gnang thabs gnang na rgyal khab phan tshun gnyis ka'i mthun lam gyi rtsa ba dang tshong pa rnams la dka' ngal mi yong ba zhig mi 'byung ngam de yang phyi nas dngul chas rigs rgyal khab tu 'byor na rgyal khab rang du thugs phan gsos yong gnas kyang dngul rigs phyi yong rnams bkag thabs mdzad don ni sgo khral thog nas rgyal khab la sku gyong chen po chags pa las de ltar mdzad pa min nam | yang gus pa'i bsam 'char ni | rgyal khab rang du 'gro rgyugs gtong len chog pa'i dngul ṭam dper na bod kyi srang sgor dang bcu sgor ṭam dkar la sogs pa khyer tshong chog gi 'dug na | bod kyi dngul rdog la sogs pa'i dngul chas rigs tshang ma srang 3 ṭam dkar par 'debs thog 'grem spel gnang na rgyal khab kyi mi dmangs la phan khyab che khar phyir 'don byas rung ka kor med pa zhig mi 'byung ngam ha cang gi rmong 'char du bkod par nongs pa mchis na bzod par mjod cig | deng srang sgor rer dbyin sgor 1 dang a na 10 re byed kyi yod skad || Tibet Mirror 16 (11), 9-10.

and customs duties. It is said that additional 90 loads [~ 17,290 kg] are to arrive in Kalimpong from Tibet without restrictions.

Furthermore, from the traders → We wonder if what has been previously confiscated – the Chinese silver imported without a permit and [that] bought and stored here [in Kalimpong] – will be immediately returned without having to pay customs duties or [encounter] legal punishment. Otherwise, [that] might damage the trade agreements and the harmony between Tibet and India; we [therefore] wonder whether it would not be best to take an immediate decision.[89]

Again, Babu Tharchin attempted to bridge legal-cultural differences by elucidating the matter of permits and fees to his readership, most of which consisted of Tibetan traders operating along the Lhasa-Kalimpong route. From the *Tibet Mirror*, issue dated February 1949:

About Chinese silver → According to what has been published in previous issues, it is not possible to export Chinese silver to India without previously asking a permit [in] India to the bank known as "Reserve Bank", but recently some traders have secretly exported Chinese silver and the like for sale to India without a permit and to the few from whom [goods] have been confiscated, these will be returned with a slight customs fee and a ten percent fine. If it is true what it is said, that, to keep in line with the rules as they appeared in the bulletins from the Indian bank published on newspapers and folios, at the time of confiscating most of the silver, there were many legal acts such as punishments, imprisonment and so on, it seems that there would be a great deal of issuing orders nowadays.[90]

China's hyperinflation and India's strong rupee heavily affected Tibetan petty traders, who witnessed a progressive depreciation of their own currency. The business circles in Kalimpong followed with concern the market fluctuations across the border, to the extent that arguments in favour of a pegged exchange rate began to circulate and were even endorsed by Babu Tharchin himself in the May issue of his newspaper:

The exchange rate of rupees in Tibet → Nowadays, it is heard that in Phari for each rupee one gets 4 *sang* and 3 *sho*; it is said that it will get higher than that. Due to the increase and decrease of the exchange rate of rupees, traders may heavily gain or loss. We wonder: would it not be very smart if our country ordered to fix the exchange rate so that it did not fluctuate? Since the government and the banks cannot control the market price of silver in China, this causes great difficulties to petty common traders. Yet, since it is not a peaceful time in China, it seems that they have no power to

---

[89] *ka sbug gi gnas tshul | lha ldan gzim tsha rong nas snga lo dbyin lo 1947 zla ba 10 pa'i nang bod nas rgya gar du rgya dngul 'dren 'khyer chog pa'i pase zhu rgyur 'bras spyi brgyud rgya gar gzhung la snyan seng zhu gnang mdzad yod 'dug kyang pase gnang son ma byung gong phag ri tsha rong las byed nas pase gnang son byung yod gsha' ha thal gyis rgya gar du rgya dngul do bcu tham pa gtong thal byung bar brten rgya gar gzhung gi sgo khral las khungs kyi sku tshab dang pu li si bcas kyis pase med par 'khyer ba 'os min zhes bkag dkyil byas pa de bzhin da lam rgya gar gzhung nas rgya dngul do brgya tham pa rgya 'dren chog pa'i pase gnang son byung 'dug pa bzhin gong gsal do bcu tham pa dbyin zla 11 tshes 25 nyin ka sbug khrims khang nas ka [*bka'] nyes dang sgo khral sogs med par phyir sprod gnang 'dug | 'phros do 90 tham pa yang bod nas ka sbug tu bkag 'gegs med pa 'byor yod 'dug pa'i gnas tshul ||*

gzhan yang tshong pa khag nas | lag 'khyer pase med par rgya dngul 'khyer yong ba dang | 'di ga rang du snga dus nas nyos bsags byas pa 'dzin bzung byas 'dug pa 'di dag ring min sgo khral bka' nyes sogs sprod ma dgos par phyir log gnang mi yong ngam snyam | de min rgya bod tshong lam la 'thus shor khar mthun lam la'ang 'thus shor yong srin na 'phral du thugs thag gcod na gang legs yong snyam || Tibet Mirror 17 (3), 3

[90] *rgya dngul skor | sngon du gsar 'gyur khag tu bkod gsal ltar rgya gar ri dzarba sbeng zhes pa'i dngul khang nas sngon du lag 'khyer mi zhus par rgya dngul sogs rgya gar du 'don tshong mi chog ces kyang | bar lam tshong pa khag nas gsang stabs su lag 'khyer med par rgya gar du dngul 'don tshong byed rgyu yin pa 'ga' zhig 'dzin bzung rnams la nye sngon sgor brgya'i thog sgor 10 sgo khral dang bka' nyes phran bu bcas slod bkrol byung 'dug | | rgya gar gzhung gi dngul khang nas sngon du gsar shog dang shog lhe rtsa tshig spel gsal ltar gyi bka' khrims la cha gnas gnang ba yin na ha lam dngul 'bor gzhung bzhes kyi khar nyes chad btson 'jug la sogs pa'i khrims lugs mang po zhig yod skad bden na da lam ha cang bka' yang gnang tshod 'dug pa'i gnas tshul || Tibet Mirror 17 (5), 10.*

control the market prices; we wonder whether it would not be good to stabilise the market prices in those countries that are peaceful.[91]

Regardless of Tibetan small traders' anxieties over the purchasing power of *sang* against rupee, no pegged exchange rate was adopted and, in the months following the PRC's encroachment on Tibet, the tide of silver coins smuggled across the border surged to unprecedented levels, due to the PLA's rising demand for essential supplies. In compliance with Mao's "gradualist" strategy, the soldiers were prohibited requisitioning of foodstuff and materials, which were to be purchased at market value (Goldstein 2007, 183). The injection of large quantities of silver coins in the local economy increased exponentially with the quartering of thousands of PLA troops in the urban areas of Central Tibet in the late months of 1951. As food and essential goods found their way, legally and illegally, from India, a steady flow of Chinese currency streamed down across the border in the opposite direction.

In the economic report forwarded by the Indian Mission, Lhasa, on May 9, 1950, Hugh E. Richardson, at the time Officer in Charge, informs the Political Officer in Sikkim Harishwar Dayal that

> [t]he Tibetan government is said to be drawing on their accumulated reserves of silver to pay part of their expenses. Their method of securing rupees when required to meet external expenditure is to sell silver to traders and officials.[92]

The report above touches upon the challenge of distinguishing illegality from legality in relation to their legitimacy. As we have seen in the course of the present study, the conceptual ambiguity about legality and illegality particularly emerges in "liminal" areas, where political, social, and economic conditions are in constant flux, and the same notion of what is (il)legal/(il)licit is situational. The issue of legality *vs* legitimacy of silver imports to India was clearly the bone of contention between Indian legislators and Tibetan traders. The border here functions as a watershed between two legislative and social systems: by selling silver for rupees, the Tibetan government indirectly fostered its illegal export to India. The licitness of the action (i.e. sale of silver) in the eyes of the "interfacing" actors (i.e. cross-bordering Tibetans) contributed to their willingness to break the law of the country in which they operated (i.e. India).

Between 1950 and 1952, large quantities of silver coins – both Tibetan *tamka* and Chinese *dayang* – were seized in Kalimpong in contravention of the Indian import regulations. In the summer of 1950, the Tibet Liaison Officer diffused an official bulletin elucidating the correct procedure to be followed.[93] In a concerted effort to educate the trading communities, the document, reported in full hereafter, was

---

[91] *bod du sgor mo'i 'dza' 'phar | deng go thos su phag khul sgor rer dngul srang bzhi dang zho gsum byed mus | da dung de las 'phar bzo yod skad | sgor thang 'phar chag byung rkyen tshong par mkhe gyong che ba yong srid | der brten rgyal khab rang nas 'phar chag med pa'i thang gzhi nges brtan gyi bka' khyab gnang na cang drag pa mi yong ngas snyam rgya nag tu rgya gzhung dang dngul khang khag nas dngul gyi thang gzhi la bdag dbang ma thub stabs mi ser tshong pa dmangs la dka' ngal chen po byung 'dug || 'o na kyang rgya nag tu dus bde min gyis thang gzhir dbang thub tshod mi 'dug kyang dus bde'i rgyal khab khag tu thang gzhi nges brtan gnang bde zhig med dam || Tibet Mirror*, 17 (8), 4.

[92] National Archives of India, External Affairs, R&I Branch, File No. 3(17)-R&I/50, Memorandum No. 3(13)-L(50).

[93] Officer especially appointed for commercial transactions and directly subordinate to the Government of India, the Tibet Liaison Officer had the task of supervising the export of goods, in particular cotton piece-goods and yarn, from India to Tibet (Provisional Parliamentary Debates. 1950 (1st February to 13th March 1950), 658-659).

taken up by two local newspapers, the *Himalayan Times*[94] and the *Tibet Mirror*, the latter providing a translation for its Tibetan readership.[95]

> IMPORT OF CURRENT SILVER COINS FROM TIBET → In view of the ban placed by the Tibetan government on the export of Tibetan current coins from that country, as well as in pursuance of the Government of India's own policy of controlling imports of silver from abroad, the Government of India have issued a notification prohibiting the import into India from Tibet without proper permission, of any silver coin which is current in that country. In future such coin may be imported only on licenses issued by the Reserve Bank of India on payment of the usual license fee. Application for such licenses should be made to the Reserve Bank of India through the Indian Mission in Lhasa or the Political Officer of Sikkim, Gangtok. Before recommendation of such applications it will be ascertained that the Tibet government has agreed to the proposed export of coins. Those concerned can ask for any information if necessary and submit their application through my office.
>
> Sd/ - S. L. Dewan,
> Tibet Liaison Officer.
> Kalimpong.[96]

Despite the efforts to counteract the unauthorised import of silver coins into Indian territory, confiscations of legal tender registered a conspicuous increase in the latter months of 1951 and the first part of 1952, an upward tendency recorded in local newspapers as well. The issues of the *Himalayan Times* still available for the period in question depict an extremely active borderland, wherein non-organised smugglers and dealers operated, either individually or in concert with one another, to gain the maximum profit. Currency trafficking was run by Tibetan transients, usually Amdowas or Khampas, in the form of petty smuggling: inconspicuous quantities of silver coins were hidden among personal items and carried across the border undeclared.[97] Once in Kalimpong, the money was either directly injected into the black market through commodity purchases or handed to local Indian fences, who handled considerable amounts of foreign currency at any time.[98] The following excerpts from two issues

---

[94] An English-language periodical published by Suresh Candra Jain in Kalimpong, the *Himalayan Times* run from 1947 to 1963. All the existing issues have been digitised within the project "Kalimpong as a 'Contact Zone': Encounters between Tibet and Western Modernity in the Early 20th Century" (Cluster of Excellence "Asia & Europe", University of Heidelberg) and made available online at https://digi.ub.uni-heidelberg.de/diglit/himalayan_times.

[95] "Verdict on importing Tibetan *tamka* coins in India → When the Tibetan government ordered that it is not allowed to export silver Tibetan *tamka* and the like for sale, the Indian government also passed a verdict on the export of silver for sale from foreign countries in India, and now the Indian government diffused a bulletin with the [following] meaning: no one is allowed to import silver or *tamka* coins and the like from Tibet to India without a permit, although it is possible to ask for a permit after paying the customary taxes to the bank called Reserve Bank through the offices of the Indian government in Lhasa or the Political Officer in Sikkim. This is what is written in the bulletin that was distributed" (*bod gzhung nas bka' rgya gnang don bod kyi dngul ṭam sgor sogs phyir 'don tshong mi chog pa'i khar rgya gar gzhung nas kyang phyi rgyal khag nas rgya gar du dngul 'don 'tshong la bkag bsdoms yod pa bzhin du da lam rgya gar gzhung nas rtsa tshig 'grem spel dgongs don du | bod nas rgya gar du bod kyi dngul lam ṭam sgor sogs lag 'khyer med par 'don 'dren mi chog kyang lha ldan du yod pa rgya gar gzhung gi yig tshang las khungs sam 'bras spyi blon chen brgyud ri zarbe sbeng ke (RESERVE BANK) zhes pa'i dngul khang du lam srol bca' khral 'jal nas lag 'khyer zhu chog pa yin zhes pa'i rtsa tshig 'grem spel gnang 'dug pa'i gnas tshul || Tibet Mirror*, 18 (8), 8

[96] *Himalayan Times*, XLVI, issue dated July 2, 1950.

[97] Instances of such a trend were also recorded by René de Nebesky-Wojkowitz during a trip from Kalimpong to Rongpu in late 1951: "A few other men in uniform, surrounded by cursing muleteers, were busily engaged in searching the packs of a Tibetan caravan that had come from the direction of Gangtok. They prodded the bales of wool hanging on the flanks of the animals with long iron rods, to make sure no other goods were hidden inside the wool. One of the policemen explained to me that many Tibetans, working for Marwaris, try to smuggle large quantities of old Chinese silver coins into India" (1956, 125-126).

[98] As concluded by Peter Reuter in his study of the criminal substructure of illegal markets, "numerous purely economic consequences, 'invisible hand' factors, lead to illegal markets being served by localized,

of the *Himalayan Times*, dated December 23, 1951 and March 9, 1952 respectively, provide valuable insights on the matter:

> SMUGGLING The art of smuggling is varied and ingenious and articles range from nylons and scents in other parts of the world to sugar and Chinese dollars on this frontier. Recent largest detections by the Excise and Land Custom was 2,500 dollars while sugar seized by the Indian Frontier Police at Rangpo was 53 boxes which were innocently marked "candles". Detection is difficult and to catch a smuggler one has to be smart and work in co-operation with a number of agents, more crudely known as "informers" without whom all smuggling would largely go undetected. It is estimated by people in the know, that actual detections are only a small part of the amount actually smuggled, and in recent weeks well over 1,000 maunds [~ 37,324 kg] of sugar have crossed into Tibet on account of the high prices prevailing there, while Chinese dollars smuggled into Kalimpong is valued at one lakh rupees. The Chinese and Tibetan authorities in Tibet are also against Chinese dollars, which have a high silver content, from being removed outside Tibet, and rules have been passed to prevent this being done. But the profit motive being strong, smuggling continues. Tibetans who risk bringing Chinese dollars to Kalimpong are assured of a fair price in rupees which of late have been becoming scarce in Tibet, and these rupees are alter used to buy consumers goods for return journey to Tibet, while agents here who buy the dollars melt these down to silver, and when the market is favourable, sell the bullion at a profit. Thus all operating in the smuggling are happy, the only ones who are perturbed are the officers who have to be on the lookout on this long and intricate frontier for the smugglers.

> DOLLAR SMUGGLING In one of our recent issues, we devoted this column in dealing with various forms of tricks followed by the smugglers operating on the Indo-Tibetan border. Our obvious intention was to emphasize the difficulty of the Enforcement Branch and Excise & Land Custom Department in detecting the offender. That was an aspect of the issue. A fair treatment of the subject, however, requires a careful analysis of the methods adopted by the other side, namely the Enforcement Branch and the Excise and Land Custom department, who are jointly responsible in carrying out the law against this crime. The question that is assailing our mind is "how the false cases of seizure are dealt with and what is the remedy for the victim?" Recently our Intelligence Correspondence has brought us shameful stories of victims of false seizure or of inordinate delay by the Excise & Land Custom department to dispose of petty cases. What is more regrettable, in both cases the victims are petty Tibetan traders quite innocent of the Indian law. It has been reported the Excise & Land Dept. and Enforcement Branch indulges in indiscriminate seizure either in their overenthusiasm to show their efficiency or justify their existence. They may also be lacking the human understanding of the consequences that will follow such indiscriminate seizure. Since the Excise and Land Custom Dept. will take 6 months to eight months, as sufficiently long period for a work which ordinarily should not take more than ten minutes. The offender can be fined on the spot a ten percent duty of his illegal smuggled Tibetan silver or Chinese dollars. But instead the alleged offender is kept waiting as long as eight months with the result that he is driven to begging on the streets or live on community charity. The wretched trader is deprived of his entire capital, may be the sale proceeds of his own land or the entire savings of his long years of servitude to his master. The general public is expected to appreciate a strict sense of duty on the part of the Government employees. But the sense of duty which is not couple with a sense of judgment and proper understanding of others' troubles may lead to foolery or inefficiency. Red-tapism has reached the limit in all government departments. The deeds and misdeeds of the Excise and Land Customs department remind us of the misery of the frog in the Aesop's Fable story and its pitiful utterance, "What is sport to you is death to us".

As illustrated above, police misconduct, rough justice, and bureaucratic vacuums were the ugly sides of crime-fighting – a short circuit that, cascading through the sensitive micro-environment of borderland areas, affected their socio-economic balance and compromised the same legitimacy claimed by the state. It is at its margins, in fact, that the latter is more fragile: as van Schendel and Abraham assert, "individuals and social groups that systematically contest or bypass state controls do not simply

---

fragmented, ephemeral, and undiversified enterprises" (1983, 130-131). In other words, in crime less is more, as high sums of money increase visibility, thus attracting unwanted attention from competitors and/or regulators (Naylor 2009, 238).

flout the letter of the law; with repeated transgressions over time, they bring into question the legitimacy of the state itself by questioning the state's ability to control its own territory" (2005, 14). Unable to counteract open violations of their boundaries, governments may encourage a dangerous escalation of violence: muscular law-enforcement and order-maintenance perturb the equilibria on the ground, creating new pockets of resistance and enhancing the subversive power of illegal economies.[99] A less confrontational stance would make it possible to embrace, and therefore diffuse, potentially threatening informal institutions: state forbearance, whereby "smuggling is framed as an informal subsidy to the borderlands", may in fact go a long way towards "buying social peace" (Gallien 2018, 20).

Hapless Tibetans were not the only ones who had to grapple with increased policing control – on the contrary, quite a few Indians experienced at first hand the government's tightening grip over cross-border activities. As reported in the *Himalayan Times*, the judicial course could take months, if not years, especially if disputes were challenged in higher courts, as in a case that involved an Indian firm and a Tibetan petty trader over the calendar year 1950-51. The events are reported below as they were recounted in the High Court of Calcutta in 1965, following the appeal filed by the defendants:[100]

Sriram Jhabarmull (Kalimpong) Ltd. v. Commissioner of Income-tax [Calcutta High Court (18 Mar 1965)]

Case No. Income-tax Reference No. 77 of 1960
Judges: G. K. Mitter
**   S. A. Masud, JJ.**
Acts: Section 66(2) of the Income-tax, 1922

Masud, J.: — The facts in this reference under **section 66(2) of the Income-tax Act, 1922**, as stated as follows:

The assessee, a limited liability company with its registered office at Kalimpong, carries on substantial business at Kalimpong with Tibetan traders in the purchase and sale of wool and textiles. The assessment year under consideration of this reference is the year 1950-51 and the corresponding year of account is 2006 R.M. In the year of the account, a sum of Rs. 70,000 was found credited in the assessee's books of account in the name of a Tibetan, Kunjo Amdo Bhutia. The assessee explained this cash credit as sum deposited by Kunjo Amdo who being an illiterate and simple Tibetan did not believe in doing business through banks. The Income-tax Officer did not accept the assessee's explanation as to the genuineness of the alleged deposit of Rs. 70,000. On appeal before the Appellate Assistant Commissioner, Kunjo Amdo gave evidence on 9th April 1957. The Appellate Assistant Commissioner found his evidence unsatisfactory and dismissed the assessee's appeal. Thereafter, the matter went up to the Appellate Tribunal who also dismissed the assessee's second appeal. On the facts set out above, the following three questions are referred to this court:

(1). Whether, on the failure of the depositor to satisfy the income-tax authorities about the nature of the sums and the source from which he came in possession thereof, the Income-tax Tribunal was justified in drawing an inference that this amount represented the undisclosed profits of the company assessable for the year 1950-51?

(2). Whether, on the facts and circumstances of the case, the said Tribunal erred in law in finding that the onus of proof lay on the petitioner to prove that the said item of cash credit which stood in the name of a third party was in fact not the petitioner's income?

---

[99] In his study of contraband along the Anglo-Dutch boundary in Southeast Asia, Tagliacozzo timely reminds us the more subversive facets of smuggling, not rarely expression of grassroots acts of resistance against state-formation processes: "[a]long some of these borders, contrabanders actively contested the expansion of these states, refusing to relinquish older trading patterns, or more insistent still, establishing new ones based on new political realities on the ground" (2005, 371).

[100] The Indian judiciary system presents a hierarchical structure of courts, formed, from top to bottom, by the Supreme Court (state level), the High Court (regional level), and the lower courts (district and village levels). I could not find, as yet, any appeals filed to the High or Supreme Courts by Tibetan defendants: it is plausible that any advantage gained in challenging a judgment in higher courts and being absolved by the charges did not offset the time and money spent in doing so.

(3).   Whether the Tribunal should have held that, in the facts and circumstances of this case, the burden of proof lay upon the income-tax authorities to show that the item of cash credit was really a part of the petitioner's income?

2. The learned counsel for the assessee, Mr. Tarun Bose, has submitted before us that his client has given a good explanation as to the source and nature of the said cash credit amounting to Rs. 70,000 and, as such, the assessee has discharged the onus of proving that the said amount belonged to a third person and, as such, could not be assessed as the assessee's income.

3. Mr. Bose has stated that the evidence given by Kunjo Amdo Bhutia, a Tibetan trader, is a possible and believable story and it cannot be rejected by the department without some positive evidence. According to Mr. Bose, these Tibetan traders are persons who bring raw materials from Tibet to Kalimpong carrying them on the shoulders of mules. They did not believe in doing transactions through banks as they could not sign their names in any Indian language. Various certificates were produced before the Income-tax Officer to show that, in the peculiar circumstances of the case, the assessee acted as bankers for Kunjo Amdo. The clear case of the assessee was that the said sum of Rs. 70,000 was deposited by Kunjo Amdo with him on April 7, 1949. This amount was supposed to be the sale proceeds of wool brought by Kunjo Amdo from Tibet to Kalimpong, and Kunjo Amdo, according to the assessee's case, got back the money through cheques on the Central Bank of India Ltd., at Kalimpong. According to Mr. Bose there was nothing unusual or unnatural in such explanation and the revenue authorities should not have rejected such explanations.

4. In our opinion, Mr. Bose's contention cannot be accepted in the facts and circumstances of this case. It is not correct to say that as soon as the initial burden of proof on the part of the assessee is discharged, the Income-tax Officer is not entitled to reject the assessee's explanation without some other positive evidence falsifying the assessee's case. It cannot be true that any possible explanation which an assessee puts forth for clarifying the source and the nature of a cash receipt must have to be accepted by the Income-tax department nor can it be lawfully urged that the Income-tax Officer can arbitrarily reject the assessee's explanation. A dogmatic assertion on the part of either the assessee or the revenue authorities cannot determine the issue. Objectively it must be found out that the assessee's explanation suffers from inherent infirmity or is inconsistent with more reliable evidence adduced by the department, before the assessee's explanation is rejected. The Madras High Court in P.V. Raghava Reddi v. Commissioner of Income-Tax [1956] 29 I.T.R 942., has rightly observed at page 948:

> "We do not think that the question of burden of proof can be made to depend exclusively upon the fact of a credit entry in the name of the assessee or in the name of a third party. In either case, the burden lies upon the assessee to explain the credit entry, though the onus might shift to the Income-tax Officer under certain circumstances. Otherwise a clever assessee can always throw the burden of proof on the Income-tax authorities by making a credit entry in the name of a third party either real or pseudonymous."

5. The point is now laid at rest by the Supreme Court in V. Govindarajuly Mudaliar v. Commissioner of Income Tax, Hyderabad [1958] 34 I.T.R 807 S.C. and Kale Khan Mohammad Hanif v. Commissioner of Income-tax [1963] 50 I.T.R 1 S.C. [101] Applying the principles set out in the aforesaid cases, we do not think that the assessee has discharged the onus satisfactorily in the instant case. The assessee's books of account show that there is inherent weakness in the evidence adduced by the assessee. Kunjo Amdo Bhutia is supposed to have sold wool worth Rs. 70,000 at Kalimpong and the sale proceeds had been deposited with the assessee on April 7, 1949. The only

---

[101] Both appeals concern the responsibility of the appellant to provide source of contested cash credits. The first appeal was addressed to the Supreme Court and by them dismissed with costs on September 24, 1958, as the appellant A. Govindarajulu Mudaliar failed to provide credible explanation for the accruement of Rs. 136,600 over the fiscal period 1945-1948. As such, the Department of Income-tax treated the amount in question as concealed income, a course of action ratified at levels of justice. Full text of the sentence available at https://indiankanoon.org/doc/922036/ [accessed on February 29, 2020]. The second appeal was addressed to the Supreme Court and by them dismissed with costs on February 8, 1963, as the appellant Kale Khan Mohammad Hanif failed to explain either the source of a specific taxable income (totalling Rs. 91,875 for the fiscal period 1945-1948) or, in case of disputed liability for tax, the reason for it to be exempted from taxation. As in the prior case, due to the impossibility to present satisfactory proof as to the source of credits, it was inferred, at all levels of justice, that these were an income of undisclosed sources. Full text of the sentence available at https://indiankanoon.org/doc/231208/ [accessed on February 29, 2020].

person to whom Kunjo Amdo sold wool are Kedarmull, Kalooram and the assessee. According to him 300 bharis[102] were sold to Kalooram and 200 bharis to Kedarmull and another 300 to the assessee. In the books of account of the assessee we find two sums of money, Rs. 34,459-6-6 and Rs. 1,780-1-3, credited December 19, 1949, and January 5, 1950, as the price of 227 bharis of wool and 14 bharis of wool, respectively. There is no evidence that wools were sold to the assessee or any other person prior to April 7, 1949. Thus, how the sale proceeds would amount to Rs. 70,000 and were kept deposited by Kunjo with the assessee are not clear. The amount of Rs. 70,000 was supposed to have been deposited with the assessee but no receipt for such deposit could be produced. Not only the particulars of the sales were not available but Kunjo stated that he did not keep any account. Further, according to Kunjo, cheques were encashed by himself personally from the Central Bank of India Ltd. and yet is was found out, on enquiry, that the cheques were encashed by the employees of the assessee. This fact shows that Kunjo has been brought to give false evidence to support the assessee's case. Apart from the oral statement of Kunjo, there is not one single document to substantiate his story. Under these circumstances, the Tribunal has rightly held that the assessee has failed to prove the genuineness of this deposit and the department was justified in bringing the amount to tax.

6. For the reasons stated above, the answers to the questions are given as follows:
Question No. 1 — Yes.
Question No. 2 — No
Question No. 3 — No. The assessee shall pay the costs of this reference to the respondent.
Mitter, J.: — I agree.[103]

The overlapping of interests made connivance among different social actors not only possible but essential. Tibetans operating across the border – be they transient contractors or permanent settlers – challenged the controls, bypassing the Indian quotas and conveying foreign silver coins into Kalimpong. Indian nationals engaged actively in the illegal sector, either providing a legitimate front to black market operations or recruiting disenfranchised individuals as dummies in money-laundering operations.

The violent side of illegal economies: prostitution, robbery, and assault

Regulated by informal institutions, illegal economies fall outside the protection of rights provided by the state: the absence of third-party enforcement and close association between earning, spending, saving or investing illicit gains increment the propensity that participants may have to advance or defend their economic interests by violent means (Naylor 2009, 231).

There are many forms of economically motivated crimes, and even more degrees in which violence may be implemented. In the context of mid-20th century Kalimpong, these could go from actions that required no direct physical violence – as was the case of illegal competition practised by Chinese settlers to discourage newcomers or intimidation and bribery used by Tibetan muleteers to force the hand of policing officers at checkpoints – to extreme anti-social behaviour, in the likes of aggravated assault, robbery, and manslaughter.

Starting from 1951, violent crimes began to be reported with increasing frequency in Kalimpong – in December of that year, a pair of Tibetan traders led a punitive expedition against a local shop-owner, guilty in their eyes of business misconduct.[104] From the pages of the *Himalayan Times*, issue dated December 16, 1951:

---

[102] Mixed clips of Tibetan wool (white and coloured, fine and coarse) were twisted into ropes and pressed into "bharis", bales weighing approximately 80 pounds (~ 37 kg) each, suitable for mule transport. See "Crisis in wool trade in Kalimpong", piece written by Suresh Chandra Jain for the *Himalayan Times*, issue dated April 20, 1952.

[103] As available at https://www.casemine.com/judgement/in/56095f0fe4b01497112c9580#

[104] Violence and illicit trade always cross in borderland regions. Here, local history, culture, and geography inevitably converge to create peculiar contexts of overlapping interests, alliances, and obligations – liminal spaces in which violence ebbs and flows, often in reaction to state policies. To understand the intertwined

SUGAR SMUGGLING Two irate Tibetans last night entered the shop of Ratey Kaiyah and demanded from the merchant a refund of money paid for sugar as they alleged the merchant was responsible for the sugar, a consignment of twenty mule loads, reaching the Tibetan border safely, but the consignment has been seized by the Sikkim State Police at Gnatong checkpost seven miles from the border. The merchant denied any knowledge of the transaction and the Tibetans partially wrecked his shop by breaking his clock. The Tibetans now face a charge of trespass.

Outside externally enforced regulatory system, interpersonal violence may easily become an accepted conduct of social interaction, even more so in a culturally diversified milieu wherein different *ethoi* collide. The Indian law prohibited the recourse to violence, yet the social actors in question clearly considered it to be an (if not, *the*) appropriate reaction to the violation of an agreement. Much like other practices performed within informal institutions, physical aggression was a socially licit praxis, against which the restrictions of the law came up.

Sites of contradictions and tensions, borderlands are, by their own nature, witnesses of interpersonal and inter-group clashes. The imposition of a legal system by a central state does not go unchallenged: as sides of the same coin, "lawmaking and lawbreaking evolv[e] antagonistically, recursively, and symbiotically" (Thai 2018, 24). As pointed out by van Schendel and Abraham, "[t]he law, like any social category, is relational, culturally inflected, and acts asymmetrically along the contours of power and social mores" (2005, 19), and it is as such bound to be contested by and adjusted to dominant social values. A telling case of the irreconcilability of social expectation and legal outcome occurred in Kalimpong on November 6, 1952. From the pages of the *Himalayan Times*, dated November 9:

ATTEMPT TO ASSAULT CRIMINAL PESHKAR Kalimpong, Nov. 6. Two Tibetans, Duka Tshering Bhutia and his wife, were arrested today by the Kalimpong police for alleged attempt to assault Sri Thapa criminal Peshkar of the local Sub-divisional officer while working in court office yesterday. The reason as ascertained from local officials is that the Tibetan Duka Bhutia had instituted a case regarding the theft of his pig and the local sub-divisional officer dismissed the case for want of sufficient evidence. After the judgement was delivered the said Tibetan is said to have collected other relatives and proceeded to the court to take the peshkar to task as the Tibetan thought he was instrumental in the dismissal of his case. Situation grew tense and Mr. Thapa the peshkar was sent home under police escort. Apprehending further troubles and on charge of attempted assault with fatal weapons and stones the Tibetan has been arrested with his wife. His mother too is wanted by the police.

Actions like the one reported above still brought criminal sanctions, yet they remained within the confines of incidental or unpremeditated violence: despite occurring in the course of an illegal act (e.g. trespass of private property or intimidation), no physical aggression was required for its performance (Naylor 2009, 232). Generally speaking, violence varies with the type of legal violation, the nature and severity of which in turn determine the nature and severity of the penalties. The repressive and punitive force exerted by the regulators against the perpetrators influences the response of the latter to possible arrest and incarceration, thus overall increasing the level of violence, either at a perceived or a real level. As Tom Naylor correctly states, "that is tantamount to saying that society's reaction to the offence is more important that the offence itself in generating violence" (2009, 238). An example of social release of pent-up tensions, which expressed itself a violent reaction to police intervention, was reported once again in the pages of the *Himalayan Times*, on June 6, 1954:

BUSINESS ASSAULTED Kalimpong, June 4. Local police arrested Zumkyab, a Tibetan, this afternoon in the 10th mile bazar here for, it is alleged, beating a Marwari businessman in his shop. It is alleged that Zumkyab entered the shop and reminding the old Marwari occupant of an old feud

---

nexus of violence and conterband and its workings, a historical approach to its devolopment is not only desirable but necessary, as convingincly argued by Tagliacozzo (2009) for the Southeast Asian case.

of Rs. 50,000/- began beating him with hands and legs and also broke his telephone and some other furniture. Hundreds of Tibetans and local merchants assembled, Police was called, and Zumkyab was arrested. Investigations are proceeding.

Violence does not need to be manifest to be meaningful: the mere threat of physical harm may be persuasive enough. In the case described above, the focus is not on Zumkyab's aggressive behaviour, rather on the mob crowding the site of the commotion. Troublesome individuals could be quickly contained and quietly disposed of by the police, but gatherings were unpredictable and easily enflamable. Any violent attempt made to arrest the culprit had to be carefully dosed lest it triggered a reaction from the witnessing fellows.

The crimes reported so far demonstrate how the permeability of the boundary between what was sanctioned by society and what was forbidden by the state created grey zones wherein outbursts of violence were tolerated, if not expected. Rather different though were the cases in which physical aggression was instrumental in the perpetration of an illegal enrichment: predatory offences, such as aggravated robbery, were condemned by both local communities and central state as causes of intra-community destabilisation and decreased safety. Being of public interest, the apprehension of criminals was, in such cases, broadcast and sensationalised by the medias, the latter a contributing factor in influencing the common perception of policing effectiveness:

> *Namthang Robbery Echo Several Persons Arrested* Kalimpong, Jan. 6. Several persons including Tibetans and Nepalis have been taken into custody by the local police in connection with the recent robbery at Namthang Estate. It will be recalled that the robbery took place in the house of Rai Saheb Balkrishna Pradhan, landlord of the Namthang Estate in Sikkim on Dec. 15, last in which cash, jewellery and gold amounting to Rs. 50,000 were removed from his house by armed gangsters who were all masked. Rai Saheb Pradhan, a Brahamin living with him and some lady members of the house are said to have been badly assaulted and Sri Pradhan with a lady of the house is said to have been bound hand and feet by the miscreants when they were refused the key of the rooms and safe. The whole affair took place quite early in evening and at a distance of only fifty feet from the main Bazar with a dozen of shops from where no help could be obtained. The robbing party was traced as far as Tarkhola from where they are supposed to have taken the road toards Khalukhop. Both the Sikkim and Darjeeling S.P.s are conducting vigorous enquiries and a special officer has been placed in charge of the investigation. Besides making certain arrests some of the robbed are also reported to have been recovered.[105]

Crime, in any form, threatens state authority and legitimacy, yet it does so in different degrees. Armed robbery and trespass of private property undermine public safety and directly impinge upon the lives of single citizens, who are therefore more vocal in requesting (and welcoming) police intervention and use of force against the culprits. Market-based offences,[106] on the other hand, represent a vaguer, less menacing threat for the general public, and a far more dangerous one for the state. Despite official perception of such form of economic crimes as a sector mainly regulated by violent means, the actual amount of physical violence varies with the type of legal violation and, in a purely theorical framework, there is nothing in the inherent logic of production, marketing, income distribution or wealth redistribution that suggests that violence is an inevitable component of the process. The absence of third-party enforcement of peaceful dispute resolution may be an incentive to resort to crude force, yet, "on-going illegal market activity likely relies more on trust between peers or extended family members" (Naylor 2009, 235), against whom threats of social repercussions are more effective than any use of

---

[105] *Himalayan Times*, XXI, issue dated January 7, 1951.

[106] Market-based offences are the form of economic crime that has the most "positive" results for legal economies, since the best part of its returns is reinjected into the market through investments, which may conceal further criminal activities (e.g. money-laundering) or be motivated by financial reasons (e.g. profit gain, assets diversification) or desire to exert territorial control through social approval.

unnecessary roughness. The potential for violence is therefore intrinsic in illegal economies, although its full expression largely depends on whether a good or service offered in a market context derives from a previous predatory crime, such as is the case for stolen or smuggled items, and on the persecutors' answer to the crimes themselves, given the strict correlation between violence of the regulators against perpetrators and the latter's reaction to possible arrest and incarceration.

Among illegal market activities, drugs and sex trades are the ones most likely to involve a certain amount of violence at all stages of the market process. As far as the Indo-Tibetan borderlands are concerned over the period in question, apart from a series of arrests in 1936, no further information on drug trafficking across the border made it to the local news, and even in those instances, the negligible amounts of opium paste seized and the disorganised nature of the distribution network – if such a term may be used for an organisation mostly formed by disenfranchised and individualistic dealers – did not require untoward use of repressive force by the regulators. Sex trafficking appears to have been even more ephemeral and fragmented, at least judging by the limited size and poor structuring of the prostitution network[107] discovered by the police in early January 1950. As reported in the *Tibet Mirror*:

> News of January 3, from Allahabad (Uttar Pradesh) or Vaishali (in Bihar) → The police have arrested twelve people: five Tibetan men, one Mongolian man, two Tibetan girls, three Gorsha (people from Nepal) girls, and one Chinese girl from Shanghai. It is said that their leader called himself "Sir" ; not only did he [claimed to] trade in women, he had also been handed over to Tibet for illicit activities in the past. Since he re-entered India, even the secret police of Calcutta were looking [for him] and, according to what is said, this "Sir" made business by bringing [in] Tibetans, disguised as women from India. Those twelve people are foreigners and are not registered in India.[108]

In the Questions & Answers session of March 10, 1951, the Indian Parliament discussed the deportation of several foreigners during the year 1950; interestingly, among them figure five Tibetans, who had been charged of women trafficking, smuggling, unauthorised entry into the country, and overstay of authorised period of stay (Provisional Parliamentary Debates. 1951 (5th February to 31st March 1951), 2119). It appears likely that these were the same Tibetans whose arrest had been reported a few months earlier in the pages of Babu Tharchin's newspaper.

When it comes to prostitution, there is a tendency to connect sex working with sex trafficking, yet nothing in the account reported above suggests that those women entered India unwillingly. Admittedly, the legal distinction between smuggling and trafficking is rather blurred and mostly lies in the agency of the migrant and the conditions under which the migration act is undertaken (Wong 2005, 87). According to the UN protocol to the resolution A/RES/55/25 dated November 15, 2000,

---

[107] At the time of his visit to Calcutta, in 1957, Tashi Tsering noted with dismay that several Tibetan women were selling themselves. In his own words: "I was surprised to find Tibetan prostitutes in India, though I suppose I shouldn't have been. […] Tibetan prostitutes at home are much subtler; their style is different. Obviously they're doing it for the money as well, but they don't make the affair seem so crass and commercial. […] I can still recall a very poor and run-down brothel in Calcutta where again I found Tibetans. The house was dark, lacked electricity, and was filthy. The poverty shocked me. I talked with the girls a bit; I felt sorry for them" (Goldstein, Siebenschuh and Tsering 1997, 50-51).

[108] *a la ha bad dam yangs pa can nas dbyin zla 1 tshes 3 nyin gsar gsal la : – bod pa mi lnga dang sog po gcig bod pa'i bu mo 2 gor sha'i bu mo 3 dang bu mo 1 rgya nag shang ha'i nas yin skad bcas mi ngo 12 la pu li sis 'dzin bzung byas 'dug cing | de tsho'i 'go byed kyi ming la sku zhabs lags brjod kyi yod ces kho rang nas brjod 'dug cing khos bud med tshong las byed kyi yod tshod ma zad sngon du khrims 'gal byas bod du rtsis sprod zhus rung yang bskyar kho pa rgya gar du 'byor par ka ta gsang ba'i pu li si nas kyang 'tshol zhib byed yi yod 'dug cing brjod skal la sku zhabs lags kyis rgya gar nas bud med la mgo skor g.yo bslus bod khrid kyi [*kyis] 'tshong gi yod skad dang | mi ngo bcu gnyis po 'di rnams phyi rgyal nas yin 'dug cing rgya gar du deb bskyel byas mi 'dug ces pa'i gnas tshul ||* Tibet Mirror 18 (4), 8.

[s]muggling of migrants shall mean the procurement, in order to obtain, directly or indirectly, a financial or other material benefit, of the illegal entry into a State Party of which the person is not a national or permanent resident. [...]

Trafficking in persons shall mean the recruitment, transportation, transfer, harbouring or receipt of persons, by means of the threat or use of force or other forms of coercion, of abduction, of fraud, of deception, of the abuse of power or of a position of vulnerability or of the giving or receiving of payments or benefits to achieve the consent of a person having control over another person, for the purpose of exploitation. [...][109]

Illuminating as these legal discriminations may be, they ignore a feature that is salient to further our understanding of 20th-century migration fluxes through the Indo-Tibetan border. In the words of Diana Wong,

the key distinction [...] between smuggling and trafficking [...] is [the one] between the service of those intermediaries [...] who primarily execute the border crossing [...] for migrants who are in active control of their own migration project (either alone or with the help of friends and relatives), and those intermediaries who recruit the migrant, organize the transport, and "sell" him to an employer [...], or are the employers themselves. (2005, 87-88).

If we adopt these sociological distinctions, the prostitution network discovered in 1950 was indeed a form of trafficking, as the Chinese man arrested by the police was the leader of the migration project and "owner" of the girls of whom he facilated the illegal entry to Indian soil. Quite different was the case for the thousands of Tibetan immigrants who found their way across the Himalayas between the 1950s and early 1960s. Far from being pawns of a structured organisation of traffickers, these people were in large part vagrants who relied on local contacts among fellow countrymen to breach the border undetected. Yet, smuggling – be it of goods or people – jeopardises the same ideas of state sovereignty and territoriality and could not be tolerated, as we shall see in the following pages.

"No man's land": vagrancy, contested citizenship, and border clashes

As early as 1947, Tibetan settlers in Kalimpong witnessed with concern the arrival of low-class countrymen who illegally crossed the border in numbers, lured by freedom from debts and servitude.[110] Those who escaped police controls often ended up living at the margins of society, sustaining themselves through begging, pandering, and theft.[111] From the *Tibet Mirror*, issue dated December 1947:

Vagrant Tibetans→ Upon the arrest of a few vagrant Tibetans, those who are permanently and legally staying in this country say that it would be best to hand them over to the Tibetan government. Similarly, there are also many jobless prostitutes who have wandered from place to place in India; it is said that, upon talks between the two governments, control will be assumed by immediately

---

[109] Article 3, Protocol to Prevent, Suppress and Punish Trafficking in Persons Especially Women and Children, supplementing the United Nations Convention against Transnational Organized Crime. Adopted and opened for signature, ratification and accession by General Assembly resolution 55/25 of 15 November 2000. As available at https://www.ohchr.org/en/professionalinterest/pages/protocoltraffickinginpersons.aspx

[110] In November 1947, sixty-six Tibetans were repatriated by the Government of India. A complete list was published on the November issue of the *Tibet Mirror* (16 (1), 8). Similar repatriations, conducted almost on a monthly basis, registered scarce success, as the same wanderers were known to attempt illegal crossing shortly after being handed over to Tibetan authorities (see *Tibet Mirror* 16 (4), 5, issue dated February 1948).

[111] In his description of fellow missionaries active in Kalimpong in the early 1950s, the British Buddhist teacher Sangharaksita mentions a certain Father Morse, allegedly "the most unpopular – not to say the best hated – man" in the area, whose leprosy clinic at Tenth Mile was located in the same "squalid building that functioned as a kind of caravanserai for Tibetans of the lowest class, including prostitutes and criminals" (1991, 268).

arresting them. If that is true, we wonder if this will not be greatly beneficial for not running into the risk [of having] a run-away of Tibetan serfs and a movement of extremely immoral countrymen.[112]

Vagrancy was not uncommon in the borderlands, yet following China's encroachment on Tibet in October 1950, an increasing number of refugees, most of whom hailing from the easternmost provinces of the plateau, sought asylum in India (Brox and Koktvedgaard Zeitzen 2017) – they were the forerunners of the tens of thousands who would eventually flee the country nine years later, together with the 14th Dalai Lama and his government. Although it would be inappropriate to talk of a refugee crisis for the period in question, the uncontrolled arrival of new dispossessed and disenfranchised elements contributed to the emergence of a general feeling of economic desperation and lack of social constraints – for many, illicit means may have been the only option against a life of misery.

The bias, also reflected in the article cited above, that sees poverty and immorality intertwined and both generating violence and social unsafety is not supported by the inherent logic of illegal economies. To borrow from Naylor,

> [t]o the extent violence does occur, the best place to look for its explanation is the societal and political context. [...] [R]egulatory violence, something that may well be intensified by misapprehensions about the level of violence prevailing in various rackets, may [...] become self-justifying by sparking a yet higher level of violence in response. (2009, 241)

In the cases examined in the present work, the outbursts of violence were sporadic and circumstantial: local police intervened with state-legitimated force, thus diffusing any potentially disruptive inter-ethnic tensions. Still, by the mid-1950s, the cosmopolitan harmony that had made of Kalimpong a trade haven began to show its first cracks: the sensitivity of borderlands to national and supranational events, the same that makes them receptive to any changes in the political and economic spheres, also triggers local adaptations, which in turn causes shifts in the social balance. To China's encroachment on Tibet (October 7, 1950) and the stationing of PLA troops in Lhasa (late 1951-early 1952) followed a period of apparent calm. Upon acceptance of the Seventeen-Point Agreement by the 14th Dalai Lama[113] and recognition by the Government of India of PRC's sovereignty over Tibet, diplomatic relations between the two superpowers (India and China) continued to be amicable, although still tainted by a certain mutual distrust. While in Lhasa the government saw with favour the gradual policy adopted by the CCP and believed in Mao's promises of religious freedom, in the easternmost regions of the plateau locals began to chafe under the Communist impositions. A growing number of Amdowas and Khampas left their native valleys to find refuge south of the Himalayan border. In January 1951, in the effort to contain illegal immigration, Indian authorities enforced the Registration of Foreigners Act, 1939 (Act no. 16), according to which foreigners were required to report their presence in and their movements across the whole country. From the *Tibet Mirror*, a joint issue dated December 1950-January 1951:

---

[112] *bod kyi mi 'khyams | bod kyi mi 'khyams 'ga' sha 'dzin gzung thog bod gzhung mchog la rtsis 'bul zhus par 'di khul tshul ldan gzhi gnas gtan chags rnams kyi sa brjod rigs su gang legs byung 'dug ces dang | da dung de mtshungs las med 'phyon ma mang po rgya gar yul gyar khag tu kha gyar nas yod pa rnams la'ang gzhung phan tshun gnyis po bka' mol thog ring min 'dzin bzung gyis rtsis bzhes mdzad kyi yod skad | la bden na rang gzhung mi rtsa phyir ma 'thor ba dang | rang rigs gang min 'chal 'gro ba sogs kyi nyes skyon mi 'byung bar phan khyab [*khyad] chen po zhig mi 'byung ngam snyam || Tibet Mirror* 16 (2), 6.

[113] The 14th Dalai Lama Tenzin Gyatso (bsTan 'dzin rgya mtsho) assumed power at the age of sixteen, on November 17, 1950. From November 1950 to July 23, 1951, the Tibetan government relocated closer to the Indian border, in Yatung. The Dalai Lama's return to Lhasa anticipated by three months his ratification of the Seventeen-Point Agreement on October 24, 1951 (Goldstein 1989, 704-813). On the Sino-Tibetan agreement of 1951, see also Shakya (2013).

On January 16, the police patrolling the border at Kalimpong diffused a bulletin saying that, according to the orders of the Indian government, from now onward all Tibetans of the settlement areas coming from Tibet will be counted among the ranks of people of the outmost borders and that by February 26 everyone must ask a permit according to what has been decided in Act no. 16, 1939 of the legislation of the outmost borders; after that date, it should be implemented according to the law.[114]

The information was further reiterated in the issue dated July 1951. Many long-term Tibetan settlers began to enquire on the possibility to be included among the indigenous minority of the Bhotias, so to have access to Indian citizenship:

It is said that, among the Tibetans whose name had been registered in the settlement lists of this district, quite a few, desiring to be included among the Indian commoners, are trying to find a way to petition for being re-included into the name registers through the Bhoḍiya Association.
Both Sikkimese and Nepalese people do not need to register, and they are denominated "Bhoḍiyā". Bhoḍiyā is [a term in] Indian language; if one translates it to Tibetan, it has no other meaning than "Tibetan" (*bod pa*). Tibetans are called in English language "Tibetan" (*ṭi sbi ṭan*), which means in Tibetan "Tibetan" (*bod pa*). It is a differentiation of mere words, Indian and English, but, in fact, it is a differentiation of Indian and Tibetan commoners.[115]

Babu Tharchin's wordplay is indicative of the legislative minefield surrounding immigration policies. The two terms indicated above – "Bhoḍiyā" and "Tibetan" – are, to all intents and purposes, "false friends"; despite their referring to the same concept, namely "Tibet" (in Tibetan, *bod*) and the people hailing from that area, they differ widely in terms of rights associated to them. Whereas the "Bhoḍiyā" (i.e. Sikkimese and Nepalese) were effectively citizens of the Republic of India, the status of the "Tibetans" was far more precarious: as registered foreigners, their residence permit was conditioned to approval and had to be renewed yearly.[116]

Regardless of Tibetan permanent residents' efforts to convince the Indian authorities of the legitimacy of their inclusion among Himalayan minorities, the tightening of security controls over immigrants continued undeterred.

INFLUX FROM TIBET INTO INDIA Kalimpong, April 9. About 3,000 lamas and 300 beggars from Tibet crossed into Indian territory through Sikkim last year, according to Indian Frontier Police guarding the eastern border. They have registered themselves as foreigners or temporary residents in India. About 10,000 Tibetans in Darjeeling district have been registered as foreigners by the

---

[114] *nye sngon yin zla dang po'i tshes 16 nyin ka sbug sa mtshams mig lta'i pu li si'i las khungs nas rgya gar gzhung gi bka' dgongs ltar slad phyin bod nas phebs mkhan 'di khul gzhis chags bod mi tshang ma phyi rgya'i mi rigs kyi gras su rtsis rgyu dang | phyi rgya'i khrims lugs don tshan bcu drug pa sngon phyi lo 1939 nang gtan 'bebs ltar tshang mas in zla 2 pa'i tshes 26 tshun lag 'khyer zhu dgos rgyu | de las 'gyangs na khrims lugs ltar lag len byed rgyu yin zhes rtsa tshig bkram song ba'i gnas tshul* || Tibet Mirror 19 (1-2), 27

[115] *sngon du 'di khul gzhi chags bod mi rnams kyi ming tho deb bskyel byas gras nas mang tsam zhig gis rgya gar mi ser khongs su tshud 'dod kyis bho ḍe ya e so se shan brgyud deb bskyel ming tho phyir log zhu thabs byed kyi yod skad ||*
'bras 'brug gnyis kyi mi rnams la deb bskyel byed dgos byung mi 'dug cing | de tshor bho ḍi yā zhes ming du btags 'dug | | bho tiyā zhes pa rgya gar skad yin gshis bod skad du bsgyur na bod pa rang go rgyu las gzhan go rgyu mi 'dug | | bod pa tshor ṭi sbi ṭan zhes ming btags 'dug pa de dbyin skad yin gshis 'di yang bod skad du bsgyur na ni bod pa rang go rgyu red | rgya gar dang dbyin ji'i tshig tsam gyi dbye ba red | 'on kyang don du bod mi ser gyi dbye ba yin tshod || Tibet Mirror 19 (4), 3

[116] "In exercise of the powers conferred by Section 3 of the Foreigners Act, 1946 (31 of 1946) and Section 3 of the Registration of Foreigners Act, 1939 (16 of 1939) the Central Government is pleased to direct that any foreigner of Tibetan nationality, who enters into India hereafter shall: (a) at the time of his entry into India obtain from officer-in-charge of the Police post at the Indo-Tibetan frontier, a permit in the from specified in the annexed Schedule; (b) comply with such instructions as may be prescribed in the said permit; and (c) get himself registered as a foreigner and obtain a certificate of registration." National Legislative Bodies / National Authorities, *India: S.R.O. 1108 of 1950 Regulating Entry of Tibetan national into India, 1950*, 26 December 1950, available at: https://www.refworld.org/docid/3ae6b52e24.html [accessed 27 March 2021]

Frontier Police since the system of registration of Tibetans was introduced on January 15, 1951. According to a spokesman of the Frontier Police, Tibetan beggars, who migrated to India on their seasonal trade in winter, are not much interested in returning home this summer on account of the reported food scarcity in Tibet. About 100 Tibetans, mostly traders, are arriving in India daily across the eastern border while about 50 leave for their country.[117]

These numbers, large as they may seem, were only a drop compared to the torrent that would follow the 14th Dalai Lama's exile to India in 1959. By that time though, Kalimpong's pulling traction as trade hub and cultural melting pot had waned dramatically: amidst the tensions of the Cold War, its strategic location made it a hotbed of espionage, to such an extent that the hill station was infamously labelled by PRC's propaganda "a nest of spies".[118]

Prior to the Sino-Indian war of 1962 and the following border militarisation that signalled the definite decline of Kalimpong as a trade centre, the Indo-Tibetan borderlands experienced a growth spell that, however brief, permanently altered the local power balance. The largest Tibetan trading firms, who had controlled the wool and cotton trade since the first decades of the 20th century, struggled to maintain their monopoly as new competitors entered the market. Pushed by the PLA's demand for foodstuff and essential supplies, prices of various commodities soared. Private porters and muleteers hired their services to the best bidder, disregarding long-standing business collaborations – every man was for himself, in a reaping frenzy created by a convergence of high demand and limited supply.[119]

On the Indian side of the border, the situation was complicated by contradictory rules and regulations, applied, often on a whim, at the checkpoints. The lack of transparency and vagueness of information, symptomatic of the government's incapacity to address local demands, translated into a general lack of public confidence and into an increase of rumour spread. As it is well-known in microeconomics, (mis)information affects preferences and has a direct impact on economic variables, such as market demands and market equilibrium prices (see Kosfeld 2005). The diffusion of false rumours to fraudulently enhance or decry the price of specific commodities/services intensifies the risk of illegal institutions infiltrating the economic texture. The following excerpt from the *Tibet Mirror*, issue dated July 1953, offers a glimpse of some of the effects that unchecked rumours had on the trans-Himalayan border economy of the time:

> On Trade → Difficulties for Tibetan petty and middle-scaled traders: firstly, it is difficult to exchange money; secondly, it is difficult to get [to India] after having crossed many passes; thirdly, there is the problem of blockade lines en route. Then, as soon as all of this is over and one reaches Kalimpong, first it is necessary to go and get a permit from the permit office, then there is the registration of one's own name in the list and the difficulties in buying the goods; it is possible to find a place where to buy things but one has to go to the black market, and it is problematic to hire the transport. All these great expenses are meaningless after the loads of items, which are arranged in pairs of boxes, are stopped at the different checkpoints [where they are unpacked]. One is said that "on this and that occasion, for this and that reason, it is not possible to export" and [so] there are confiscations, arrests, and imprisonment. These are said to be the great difficulties experienced by petty and middle traders. Furthermore, as explained by a few traders, the rumour that the Indian

---

[117] *Himalayan Times*, XXXIV, issue dated April 6, 1952.

[118] In a Parliamentary hearing in the Lower House (Lok Sabha) on March 30 and April 2, 1959, President Nehru addressed the situation in Kalimpong, and while he dismissed the PRC's accusations of Indian collusions with Tibetan rebels, he could not deny that the hill town had been a site of intense espionage and counter-espionage since the mid-1940s (Lok Sabha Debates (April 2, 1959), 9263-9288). See also Poddar and Lindkvist Zhang (2017). For a recent study of Kalimpong as a site of espionage and counter-espionage activity between the 1940s and the 1960s, see Sen (2021).

[119] In early 1952, the situation in Central Tibet was dramatic: the food requirements for the PLA soldiers stationed in Lhasa were far beyond the supply capacity of the local government. In the summer of that year, the PRC organised the transport of 1,350 tons of rice from Kalimpong to Lhasa, in a desperate attempt to staunch the food crisis (Goldstein 2007, 244-264).

government prohibited Tibetan traders from buying commodities for export by issuing a bulletin is a misunderstanding. Not only that, there are also many claiming to have heard that the Prime Minister said not to ban to export of goods to Tibet, yet why they are making it so hard? If it was not possible to export to Tibet this and that commodities, why are the Indian traders selling as much as possible to the Tibetan traders at the highest price? Why is the Indian government not ordering the Indian traders not to sell this and that commodity to Tibetan traders? Why, at the checkpoints, on some is imposed a ban, saying [to them] "these items are not allowed to be exported", when there are others who arrive in great number in the plain of Phari without being blocked? It is said that many discussions about these matters have been held between petty and middle traders. In any case, Indian regional authorities have issued a bulletin to all traders regarding which commodities are not allowed to be exported; if one exports them, they will be seized and confiscated. The bulletin must certainly be circulated, otherwise senseless problems and losses will occur to petty and middle traders, and that will not be good.[120]

Between 1952 and 1954, many Tibetans nevertheless profited from the situation. The Bank of China, which had opened a branch office in Lhasa, granted drafts to local traders who could cash them for rupees in Kalimpong or Calcutta (Goldstein 2007, 261-262): the market was constantly injected with silver coins, a good amount of which spilled, as we have seen, into the illegal sectors. As is often the case in a market economy, both its facets – licit and illicit – benefited from the growth spell, as confirmed by the *Tibet Mirror*, July issue:

> Lately, in just one year there has been a trade greater than any we had for many years, and very busy Indian and Tibetan traders are making [both] white and black markets grow.[121]

The Indo-Tibetan borderland regions were still enjoying the aftermath of the brief economic boom brought by the PLA's stationing in Lhasa, when a new piece of positive news reached them. After long negotiations, the seeds of which had been sown at the time of the Seventeen-Point Agreement in 1951, the Republic of India and the People's Republic of China reached an arrangement over trade and transportation. The Sino-Indian treaty, signed on April 29, 1954, saw India's abandonment of the Anglo-Tibetan regulations of 1914 and the consequent forsaking of any controversial claims to territorial rights in Tibet. Trade and intercourse of India with the "Tibet Region of China" were clearly the most important features of the new agreement and promptly acknowledged as such in its first

---

[120] *tshong gi skor | bod tshong chung 'bring rnams kyi bde sdug | dang por dngul brje thob dka' ba | gnyis pa la lung mang po brgyab nas yong dka' ba | gsum pa lam bar sa mtshams khag tu bkag sdom kyi dka' ngal | de nas thar tsam gyis ka sbug tu 'byor mtshams dang po pa se'i las khung su bcar nas par len tu 'gro dgos pa | de nas ming tho deb skyel byed dgos pa | de nas tshong zog nyo dka' ba | nyos thob rung nag tshong du nyo dgos pa | de nas bdal gtong bka' ba | sa mtshams khag tu tshong zog do po bkag nas sgam dor gris rtsa ba stabs don med 'gro song che ba | la lar 'di dang 'di 'don mi chog pa red ces 'dzin bzung do dam btson 'jug byed pa sogs kyis tshong pa chung 'bring rnams la bka' ngal chen po yod skad | gzhan yang tshong pa khag nas brjod gsal la | rgya gar gzhung nas rtsa tshig 'grems spel thog bod tshong rnams nas tshong zog 'di dang 'di nyo 'don mi chog ces pa ni ma mthong | der ma zad srid blon chen pos bod 'gro'i tshong rigs la bkag sdom med gsungs skad go thos byung rung bar pas sdug po ster ba ci yin nam zhes brjod mkhan mang po dang | tshong zog 'di dang 'di bod du 'gro chog med na rgya gar tshong pas ga re don la gong chen po len nas bod tshong rnams la tshong gang thub byed kyi yod pa red | ga re'i don la rgya gar gzhung nas rgya gar tshong pa rnams la zog rigs 'di dang 'di bod tshong khag la 'tshong mi chog ces pa'i bka' rgya mi gnang ba ga re red | sa mtshams khag tu tshong zog 'don rigs mi chog pa yin zhes gzhan la bkag sdom byas rung | la lar bkag sdom med par phag ri thang du grangs med 'byor ba de dag ga re red ces tshong chung 'bring rnams kyi dbar bka' mol mang po yod skad | gang ltar rgya gar sa gnas dpon khag rnams nas tshong pa tshang mar rtsa tshig thog zog rigs 'di dang 'di zhes bya ba 'don tshong mi chog 'don na bkag sdom gzhung bzhes yin zhes 'grem spel gnang med na nges par du gnang dgos | de min tshong pa chung 'bring rnams la don med sdug po dang gyong gun 'byung ba yag po mi 'dug | Tibet Mirror* 21 (4), 4.

[121] *tshong gi rigs → deng rgya bod gnyis kyi dbar sngon du lo mang nang ma byung ba'i tshong chen po deng lo gcig nang yong gi yod 'dug cing rgya bod tshong pa rnams ha cang thugs brel chen pos dkar nag tshong las gong 'phel gnang mus su mchis pa'i gnas tshul || Tibet Mirror* 21 (4), 3.

opening lines. Based on the principle of peaceful coexistence and mutual recognition,[122] the document effectively signed the end of Indo-Tibetan direct relations and the full diplomatic recognition of China's sovereignty over the plateau.

Up to 1954, Tibet had acted with a certain degree of autonomy in the geopolitical arena of Asia: brokers between two *économie-mondes* (Spengen 2000), Tibetans travelled across borders, facilitating the transit of commodities, people, and ideas. In the wake of post-colonialism, the emergence of new independent states and their morphing into competing superpowers determined a progressive stiffening of border permeability and the clampdown on unchecked movement. In kick-starting a brief season of friendly commercial relations between China and India, the signing of the Sino-Indian trade agreement rang the death toll for any pretence at self-rule that the Tibetan government may have still harboured and signed the beginning of a new era in the borderland regions.

In spelling out the border passes regulating the authorised flow of trans-Himalayan trade and pilgrimages, the signatory members of the trade agreement deliberately omitted the eastern sector of the border:[123] a potential dispute to the Indian claim to the McMahon Line made raising the issue undesirable in view of any diplomatic reconciliation. The Sino-Indian treaty was received by the Indian press with mixed feelings. The relinquishment of long-standing privileges in Tibet – a British legacy to the Republic – was mitigated by the opening of a consulate in Lhasa in lieu of the old Indian Mission, a remnant of the imperialistic designs over Central Asia, the legality of which had been periodically questioned. Nehru himself was mildly disappointed, as his desire for a twenty-five-year treaty was frustrated by the Chinese refusal to agree to anything longer than eight years (Gupta 1974, 726). The Indian Prime Minister's suspicions towards such a half-hearted friendship proved not unwarranted: regardless of the actively amicable policy – the "Hindi-Chini bhai-bhai" – proclaimed in the mid-1950s, the profound differences between the two political systems and the tensions on border issues progressively derailed what had been an uneasy relations since its outset.[124]

The lack of references in the trade agreement of 1954 to the matter of border delimitation, especially on the eastern side, only delayed the inevitable confrontation that was due to occur. After the publication of China Pictorial's map in 1958, Nehru and Zhou Enlai engaged in a diplomatic skirmish the tone of which became dangerously belligerent. On March 31, 1959, a failed uprising against the PLA troops stationed in Lhasa turned the tables drastically: the twenty-four-year-old Dalai Lama fled to India with more than 80,000 followers in tow, to whom the Indian government grudgingly offered political asylum. Contrary to the Indian populace's heartfelt welcoming of the Tibetan spiritual leader, Nehru proved less sentimental, as he was keenly aware of the repercussions that granting legitimacy to the Dalai Lama's claim to independence would have on the already strained Sino-Indian relationships. Tensions between the superpowers rose to breaking point in August 1959, when Nehru accused the PRC of aggressive behaviour along the McMahon Line. Despite Zhou Enlai's attempts to defuse any further escalation, the Indian Prime Minister, by then cornered by his own Parliament members, refused to concede, even when the Soviet Union prodded him for an agreement.

By the end of 1961, the situation was tense. China had started a large-scale militarisation programme in Tibet, counter-acted by dispatches of military positions in Ladakh by India. War broke

---

[122] The "Five Principles of Peaceful Coexistence" were (1) mutual respect for territorial integrity and sovereignty; (2) mutual non-aggression; (3) non-interference in each other's internal affairs; (4) equality and mutual benefits; and (5) peaceful coexistence (Gupta 1974, 726; Goldstein 2007, 469-470)

[123] No reference is either made to the even more problematic western sector where the frontier of the Kashmir state lay. The PRC refused to entertain any discussion concerning the trade marts in Western Tibet on the ground that the territory in question was under dispute between India and Pakistan (Gupta 1974, 726).

[124] For an in-depth analysis of China's policy towards India and the frontier dispute, see Dai Chaowu (2017).

out on October 20, 1962, when the Chinese launched a "punitive expedition" on both the western and eastern fronts. Although victorious, Zhou Enlai was the one who urged for a treaty, yet his proposal was rejected by Nehru. Between November 15 and 19, 1962, the PLA overcame any military opposition in the contested areas, declared a unilateral ceasefire, and forwarded to the Indian government the same measures proposed in October. Defeated, the Indian army had to accept the de facto border as drawn by China, which had retreated north of the McMahon Line (Kemenade 2008, 31-42), the latter itself a contexted ground given the unyielding refusal of China to ratify the Anglo-Tibetan agreement over the Tibet-Assam border as signed by the representatives of the two governments at the Simla Conference (October 1913-July 1914). Although there have been no changes to the military status quo up to this day, the border issue remains unresolved, and incidents are periodically reported in the Indian media with buzzwords (e.g. "incursions", "intrusions" or "violations") that are at odds with the government's tendency to downplaying or outright denying these "intrusions" (Bhonsale 2018), as demonstrated by the "brawl" at the Nathu La pass on January 20, 2021.

The closure of the border in 1962 sealed the end of Kalimpong as a trade hub. Business in the hill station had indeed experienced a substantial decline since 1954, a situation largely ascribable, as we have seen, to bureaucratic disorganisation and contradictory instructions imparted to the traders by various government officials, such as the Political Officer in Sikkim, the Tibet Liaison Officer, the Sikkim State and Land Customs Officials, the Enforcement Police, and the Frontier Check Post Staff (Harris 2017b, 217-218). As early as the first months of 1958, the prospects for Indo-Tibetan trade were grim, and no delusions on the matter were harboured by the locals. From the *Himalayan Times* dated February 16, 1958:

> This season of Indo Tibet trade has been one of the worst it can be said without any hesitation. There are many reasons for this. The most important cause of this position is due to huge accumulation of goods in Tibet which are still lying undisposed. The postponement of the development plan in Tibet by the Chinese authorities can also be ascribed as one of the reasons. The quantity of Tibetan Wool which came to India was comparatively low than past few years. Although the political office at Gangtok has always been trying to help the Indian interest, the entrance of some unscrupulous businessmen and their dishonest practices have been responsible for losing good will of Tibetan traders. Due to this year's bad season already four or five concerns have been closed down and many are contemplating to do so. If the present position continues, there will be threat of a big unemployment. Traders have no uniform policy and at Kalimpong alone there are half a dozen Trade bodies. (as quoted in Harris [2017b, 217-218])

If a closed border made the cease of legal trade and movement a foreseeable consequence, the same cannot be said for the dwindling of illegal transit of goods and people that followed the militarisation of the eastern front: it is not unusual in fact for closed borders to be regulated by informal institutions through the establishment of pre-arranged exchange points (Gallien 2018, 15-16). Rather than the outcome of a closed border, the waning of exchanges across the Indo-Tibetan route has to be largely attributed to both the general weakening of the local borderlands' economies and global changes in technological transportation: motorable roads and air routes had by then shrunk the perception of space and time, substantially modifying traders' (and consumers') expectations. The closing of shops and trading firms was soon followed by the shutting down of local publishing houses: the last issue of the *Himalayan Times*, dated February 17, 1963, counts the newspaper as "another victim of the complete stoppage of the Indo-Tibet trade".

A Final Thought

From the late 18th century onwards, the valleys on either side of the Himalayan border became an active theatre of political experimentation, as local communities alternatively aided and hindered the very same nation-building processes that aimed to make of them a stable, if not static, bulwark of a centripetal polity. Due to their "in-betweenness", both literal and figurative, these unregulated, porous spaces suffered and profiteered in equal measure from the power configurations at play at a national and supranational level. Yet, the institution of borders, part and parcel of modern concepts of nation-states and starting point of my reflection on the nature of borderland regions, inevitably muddles our understanding of human mobility and commodity movements in those areas. As neatly expressed by David Ludden,

> modernity consigned human mobility to the dusty dark corners of archives that document the hegemonic space of national territorialism. As a result, we imagine that mobility is border crossing, as though borders came first and mobility second. (2003, 1062)

Flexible, filtering membranes, modern borders are geopolitical constructs that attempt to subsume under a thin line the deep heterogeneity – symbolic, linguistic, cultural, and economic – present on the ground. The often arbitrary superimposition of demarcations never goes unchallenged by the locals, who dexteriously reconfigure and replot their movements, exchanges, and contacts – "[t]he bread and butter of borderland studies" (Saxer et al. 2018, 6) – to either bypass or exploit the boundaries fixed by the nation-state, thus disregarding any forced-upon claims to territorial sovereignty, as the U.S.-based Latinos' motto – "we did not cross the border, the border crossed us" – cogently sums up (Mezzadra and Neilson 2013, ix).

This is particularly true in the context of Asian borderlands, where "cross-border interactions tend to go along with processes of exchange outside the channels set up for this purpose" (Saxer et al. 2018, 7).[125] Far from being the "God-given boundary" of Thomas H. Holdich's imaginary, the Himalayan ranges were crossed by century-old routes connecting Central and Inner Asia to the Indian subcontinent. With the opening of Tibet to British India in the aftermath of the Younghusband Expedition, the hamlet of Kalimpong quickly turned into a trade hub. The booming economic growth that characterised the history of the hill-station in the first part of the 20th century led to its becoming a "contact zone", a multicultural pot where licit and regulated trade corridors were flanked by other, illegal passageways. Although substantial, the role that Tibetans – dwellers and transients alike – played in both "white" and "black" border economies went largely unnoticed, as only few cases made the local news, the latter a factor that much reveals the complexities inherent to any discourses on licitness/illicitness in border areas.[126]

Located as they are at the "fringes" of the state, borderlands offer in fact the perfect terrain for ongoing struggles over legitimacy, as movements that defy the rules and norms of the nation-state may very well be "licit" in the eyes of those who engage in them. Whenever such fundamental social acceptability is lost though, the protection provided by customary informal institutions fades, and the actors who find themselves on the wrong side of the fence are left to their own devices, as clearly demonstrated by those, admittedly few, Tibetans who in the early 1930s were charged of drug possession and dealing.

Despite noticeable exceptions (e.g. drugs, weapons, human trafficking), most of the smuggling activities carried out across the Himalayan passes enjoyed a remarkable social licitness, to the point of being almost a "way of border life": illegal or semi-legal movement of goods and currency continued

---

[125] For a historical overview of illicit cross-border traffics in Asia, see, among others, Tagliacozzo (2005) and Thai (2018).

[126] Thai correctly cautions against a hasty assumption of a direct correlation between an increase in recorded instances of crime and an actual rise in illicit activities, questioning whether the growth in public awareness is driven by *crime* waves or *enforcement* waves (2018, 6).

in fact unabated up to the 1960s, closely tailing national and global economic trends. During WWII, Kalimpong became the bottleneck through which unlicensed supplies were funneled to China: the high level of demand stimulated interactions among local business groups, with Chinese firms, Indian shop-owners, and Tibetan muleteers networking and collaborating in a profit-driven frenzy. The commingling of interests represents a well-known facet of illegal economies, so much so that crime may be rightfully considered a catalyst for globalisation.

In the post-war years, the Indian Independence first and the Chinese encroachment on Tibet later led to an increase in illegal activities in the area of Kalimpong. The reinforcement of pre-war commodity control policies in India on one hand and the waves of hyperinflation that repeatedly hit China on the other created the perfect environment for illegal cross-border operations. Demonetised ROC silver coins, injected into the Chinese markets to counterbalance the loss of yuan's purchase power, trickled from the southwestern provinces of Sichuan and Yunnan to Tibet and from there to the Himalayan trade-hub, where they were used as payoffs for illegal transactions.

The inability of the Indian government to establish an efficient border control net betrays the contradictions intrinsic to borderlands, as local border praxes recognise no geopolitical lines. Any attempt to enforce borders as seen by state ideology by means of muscular displays is bound to trigger a short circuit that, reverberating across the sensitive micro-environments of the border areas, disrupts their delicate socio-economic balance. Whereas limited outbursts of violence may be tolerated as unpleasant yet temporary byproducts of a long-term social peace, centralised order-maintenance and indiscriminate resort to brute force threaten the same state legitimacy they aim to reinstate, paradoxically damaging healthy segments of the local economy while pushing illegal networks underground.

The resilience of illegal economies in fact ensures those operating in these sectors a certain degree of buoyancy in the face of external restrictions, be they government regulations, legal strictures or open militarisation, yet, like any other flow dynamics, their life-force depends on demand and supply. In a situation of economic standstill, it is to be expected that all sectors, licit and illicit alike, will suffer; the capacity of illegal economies to survive, and even thrive under, political clampdowns – in this case, a closed border – much rests on the strength of the informal institutions at work. As we have seen, the smuggling networks operating in the market-based economy of the Indo-Tibetan borderlands were extremely localised, fragmented, and ephemeral, mainly structured upon ethnic or customary ties that proved too feeble in the face of the socio-economic uprooting caused by the Sino-Indian clashes.

The steep drop in illegal flows across the border did not, however, translate into a complete stop: as late as 1960, smuggling of various items – wristwatches, cotton piece-goods, motor parts, petrol, sugar, tobacco – was still reported.[127] Tellingly, most of these controlled commodities transited through authorised Indian firms or Tibetan traders who used legal corridors to avoid additional security clearance. The profit illegally obtained by bypassing taxations and customs duties were once again reinjected into the legal sectors through commodities investments, the latter a cycle eventually broken by the unravelling of traditional cross-border networks in the early 1960s.

The *Tibet Mirror*, just like the *Himalayan Times*, published its last issue in 1963. The closure of what had been the main sources of information on the Tibetan community in Kalimpong fittingly acts like a watershed, marking the end of an era and the beginning of a new, more uncertain, one. Yet, transnational and transcultural connections continue here even today, as do the illicit activities of those who call these borderlands their home, regardless, and often in spite, of global policies and trends.

---

[127] National Archives of India, External Affairs, "Smuggling of controlled items of good to Tibet", File No. 1/6/NGO/60.

Acknowledgment

The present research has been conducted within the framework of the ANR-DFG funded project "Social Status in the Tibetan World". I thank Professor Charles Ramble (EPHE – PSL / CRCAO) for his suggestions and comments on the first draft of this work, and the two anonymous reviewers for their thorough assessment and thoughtful advice. My deepest gratitude goes to Dr Mingma Lhamu Pakhrin (Jawaharlal Nehru University) for her invaluable and timely assistance at the National Archives of India, and to Lynn Holt for her extreme care and dedication throughout the writing process.

The content of this work reflects solely the author's view and does not necessarily represent those of any other entity, institution, or employer to which the author is affiliated.

Archival material, National Archives of India

External Affairs, External Branch, File No. 104-X/42, "Question of import into India of silver bullion and coins etc. from Tibet. Desire of one Hopi Ghalam Rasul, a Ladakhi Mohammedan at Lhasa, to visit Mecca".

External Affairs, External Branch, File No. 104(2)-X/42, "Imposition by the District Magistrate, Darjeeling under the authority of the Government of Bengal on exports from the Darjeeling districts to Tibet and their subsequent removal. Exports from India via Sikkim to Tibet, Bhutan and China via Tibet".

External Affairs, Far Eastern Branch, File No. 683(3)-FE/44, "Trans-Tibet Route. (Supplies to China)".

External Affairs, War Branch, Progs. Nos. 42(39)-W/44 (Secret), "Censorship Interceptions --- Telegram from Wangyunbao, Lekiang to Chokochung, Kalimpong regarding smuggling of illegal goods to China via Tibet".

External Affairs, Central Asia, Progs., Nos. 504-CA/44, "Report on the Chinese at Kalimpong".

External Affairs, Central Asia, Progs., Nos. 557-CA/44 (Secret), "Report on a Trip made by Captain A.R. Allen to Kalimpong in connection with Kalimpong Securities Problem and Sino Tibetan Conmmercial activities".

External Affairs, North East Frontier Branch, File Progs., Nos. 16(3)-NEF/48, "Decision to postpone the institution of a land customs barrier between India and Tibet, and to continue the practice of restricting free transit through India to goods imported by important Tibetan personages. 2. Continuance of the enumeration posts at Gangtok and Rongli".

External Affairs, R&I, File No. 3(17)-R&I/50, "Annual and Bi-Annual Reports from Tibet".

Bibliography

Andreas, Peter. 2001. *Border Games: Policing the U.S.-Mexico divide.* Ithaca, N.Y.: Cornell University Press.

Arnold, David. 2014. "Hodgson, Hooker and the Himalayan Frontier, 1848-1850." In *The Origins of Himalayan Studies: Brian Houghton Hodgson in Nepal and Darjeeling, 1820-1858*, edited by David Waterhouse, 189-205. London: Routledge.

Arora, Vibha. 2007. "Assertive Identities, Indigeneity, and the Politics of Recognition as a Tribe: The Bhutias, the Lepchas and the Limbus of Sikkim." *Sociological Bulletin*: 195-220.

Baud, Michiel, and Willem van Schendel. 1997. "Toward a Comparative History of Borderlands." *Journal of World History* 8 (2): 211-242. Accessed January 05, 2020. https://www.jstor.org/stable/20068594.

Baumgartner, Joseph. 1981. "Newspapers as Historical Sources." *Philippine Quarterly of Culture and Society* 9 (3): 256-258. Accessed January 16, 2020. https://www.jstor.org/stable/29791732.

Baumler, Alan. 2007. *The Chinese and Opium under the Republic: Worse than Floods and Wild Beasts.* Albany, NY: State University of New York Press.

Beckert, Jens, and Matías Dewey, eds. 2017. *The Architecture of Illegal Markets: Towards an Economic Sociology of Illegality in the Economy.* Oxford: Oxford University Press.

Bello, David A. 2001. "The Chinese Roots of Inner Asia Poppy." *Cahiers d'Études sur la Méditerranée Orientale et le monde Turco-Iranien* 32 (1): 39-68. Accessed January 22, 2020. https://www.persee.fr/doc/cemot_0764-9878_2001_num_32_1_1598.

Bergmann, Christoph. 2016. *The Himalayan Border Region: trade, identity and mobility in Kumaon, India.* Switzerland: Springer.

Berounský, Daniel. 2013. "Demonic Tobacco in Tibet." *Mongolo-Tibetica Pragensia* 6 (2): 7-34.

Bertsch, Wolfgang. 2002. *The Currency of Tibet: A Sourcebook for the Study of Tibetan Coins, Paper Money and Other Forms of Currency.* Dharamsala: Library of Tibetan Works and Archives.

Bertsch, Wolfgang, and Nicholas G. Rhodes. 2010. "The Use of Cut Coins in Tibet." *The Tibet Journal* 35 (3): 19-40.

Bhonsale, Mihir. 2018. "Understanding Sino-Indian Border Issues: An Analysis of Incidents Reported in the Indian Media." *Observer Research Foundation Occasional Paper.* Accessed February 2020, 2020. https://www.orfonline.org/research/understanding-sino-indian-border-issues-an-analysis-of-incidents-reported-in-the-indian-media/.

Brass, Paul R. 2003. "The Partition of India and Retributive Genocide in the Punjab, 1946-47: Means, Methods, and Purposes." *Journal of Genocide Research* 5 (1): 71-101. Accessed February 06, 2020. http://faculty.washington.edu/brass/Partition.pdf.

Brown, Richard Harvey. 2002. "The Opium Trade and Opium Policies in India, China, Britain and United States: Historical Comparisons and Theoretical Interpretations." *Asian Journal of Social Science* 30 (3): 623-656.

Brox, Trine, and Miriam Koktvedgaard Zeitzen. 2017. "Prince Peter's Seven Years in Kalimpong: Collecting in a Contact Zone." In *Transcultural Encounters in the Himalayan Borderland: Kalimpong as a "Contact Zone"*, edited by Markus Viehbeck, 245-272. Heidelberg: Heidelberg University Press.

Cabinet Secretariat. 1957. "The Abolition of Opium Smoking in India." *Bulletin on Narcotics* (3): 1-7. Accessed January 24, 2020. https://www.unodc.org/unodc/en/data-and-analysis/bulletin/bulletin_1957-01-01_3_page002.html.

Dai Chaowu. 2017. "From 'Hindi-Chini Bhai-Bhai' to 'International Class Struggle' against Nehru: China's India policy and the frontier dispute, 1950-62." In *The Sino-Indian War of 1962: New Perspectives*, edited by Amit R. Das Gupta and Lorenz M. Lüthi, 68-84. London; New York: Routledge.

de Soysa, Indra, and Johannes Jütting. 2007. "Informal Institutions and Development: How They Matter and What Makes Them Change." In *Informal Institutions: How Social Norms Help or Hinder Development*, edited by Johannes Jütting, Denis Drechsler, Sebastian Bartsch and Indra de Soysa, 29-43. Paris: OECD Publishing.

Dirks, Nicolas B. 2002. "Annals of the Archive: Ethnographic Notes on the Sources of History." In *From the Margins: Historical Anthropology and Its Futures*, edited by Brian Axel, 47-65. Durham, NC: Duke University Press.

Donnan, Hastings, and Thomas M. Wilson. 1999. *Borders: Frontiers of Identity, Nation and State.* Oxford: Berg.

Donnan, Hastings, and Thomas M. Wilson. 2012. "Borders and Borders Studies." In *A Companion to Border Studies*, edited by Thomas M. Wilson and Hastings Donnan, 1-25. Malden, Mass.: Blackwell.

Driessen, Henk. 1999. "Smuggling as a Border Way of Life: A Mediterranean Case." In *Frontiers and Borderlands: Anthropological Perspectives*, edited by Michael Rösler and Tobias Wendl, 117-127. Frankfurt am Main: Peter Lang.

Economic Commission for Asia and the Far East. 1948. *Economic Survey of Asia and the Far East 1947.* Economic Survey, Shangahi: United Nations Publications. Accessed February 12, 2020. https://www.unescap.org/publications/economic-survey-asia-and-far-east-1947.

Economic Report 1945-1947. Department of Economic Affairs of the United Nations. 1948. *Economic Report: Salient Features of the World Economic Situation 1945-1947.* Economic Report, New York: United Nations Publications. Accessed February 12, 2020. https://www.un.org/en/development/desa/policy/wess/wess_archive/1945_1947wes_salient_features_txt.pdf.

Engelhardt, Isrun. 2011. "Reflections on the Tibet Mirror: News of the World, 1937-1946." In *Mapping the Modern in Tibet*, edited by Gray Tuttle, 205-264. Halle (Saale): International Institute for Tibetan and Buddhist Studies (IITBS).

Erhard, Franz Xaver. 2015. "Tibetan Mass Media: A Preliminary Survey of Tibetan Language Newspapers." In *The Illuminating Mirror: Tibetan Studies in Honour of Per K. Sørensen on the Occasion of His 65th Birthday*, edited by Olaf Czaja and Guntram Hazod, 155-171. Wiesbaden: Dr. Ludwig Reichert Verlag.

Fader, H. Louis. 2002. *Called from Obscurity: The Life and Times of a True Son of Tibet, Gergan Dorje Tharchin*, 3 vols. Kalimpong: Tibet Mirror Press.

Gallien, Max. 2018. "Informal Institutions and the Regulation of Smuggling in North Africa." *Perspectives on Politics* 1-29. Accessed January 09, 2020. http://eprints.lse.ac.uk/id/eprint/90957.

Gellner, David N., ed. 2013. *Borderland Lives in Northern South Asia.* Durham and London: Duke University Press.

Gellner, David N. 2013. "Introduction: Northern South Asia's Diverse Borders, from Kachchh to Mizoram." In *Borderland Lives in Northern South Asia*, edited by David N. Gellner, 1-23. Durham and London: Duke University Press.

Goldstein, Melvyn C. 1989. *A History of Modern Tibet. Volume I: The Demise of the Lamaist State, 1913-1951.* Berkeley: University of California Press.

Goldstein, Melvyn C. 2007. *A History of Modern Tibet. Volume 2: The Calm Before the Storm: 1951-1955*. Berkeley: University of California Press.

Goldstein, Melvyn C., William Siebenschuh, and Tashi Tsering. 1997. *The Struggle for Modern Tibet: The Autobiography of Tashi Tsering*. London; New York: Routledge.

Gros, Stéphane, ed. 2016. "Frontier Tibet: Trade and Boundaries of Authority in Kham." *Cross-Currents: East Asian History and Culture Review* 19. Online. https://cross-currents.berkeley.edu/e-journal/issue-19

Gros, Stéphane, ed. 2019. *Frontier Tibet: Patterns of Change in the Sino-Tibetan Borderlands*. Amsterdam: Amsterdam University Press.

Gupta, Karunakar. 1974. "Hidden History of the Sino-Indian Frontier I—1947-1954." *Economic and Political Weekly* 9 (18): 721-726. Accessed February 23, 2020. https://www.jstor.org/stable/41497054.

Hall, Thomas D. 2005. "Borders, Borderlands, and Frontiers, Global." In *New Dictionary of the History of Ideas*, edited by Maryanne Cline Horowitz, vol. 1, 238-242. Detroit: Charles Scribner's Sons.

Hämäläinen, Pekka, and Samuel Truett. 2011. "On Borderlands." *Journal of American History* 98 (2): 338-361. Accessed January 05, 2020. https://doi.org/10.1093/jahist/jar259.

Harris, Tina. 2008. "Silk Roads and Wool Routes: Contemporary Geographies of Trade Between Lhasa and Kalimpong." *India Review* 7 (3): 200-222.

Harris, Tina. 2017a. "The Mobile and the Material in the Himalayan Borderlands." In *The Art of Neighbouring: Making Relations Across China's Borders*, edited by Martin Saxer and Juan Zhang, 145-166. Amsterdam: Amsterdam University Press.

Harris, Tina. 2017b. "Wool, Toothbrushes, and Beards: Kalimpong and the 'Golden Era' of Cross-Border Trade." In *Transcultural Encounters in the Himalayan Borderlands: Kalimpong as a "Contact Zone"*, edited by Markus Viehbeck, 205-222. Heidelberg: Heidelberg University Press.

Hegre, Håvard, John R. Oneal, and Bruce Russett. 2010. "Trade Does Promote Peace: New Simultaneous Estimates of the Reciprocal Effects of Trade and Conflict." *Journal of Peace Research* 47: 763-774.

Helfgott, Jacqueline B. 2008. *Criminal Behavior: Theories, Typologies and Criminal Justice*. Los Angeles; London: Sage.

Herrog, Lawrence A. 1990. *Where North Meets South: Cities, Space, and Politics on the U.S.-Mexico Border*. Austin: Center for Mexican American Studies.

Holdich, Thomas H. 1901. *The Indian Borderland, 1880-1900*. London: Methuen.

Holland, Alisha C. 2015. "The Distributive Politics of Enforcement." *American Journal of Political Science* 59 (2): 357-371.

Holland, Alisha C. 2016. "Forbearance." *American Political Science Review* 110 (2): 232-246. https://doi.org/10.1017/S0003055416000083.

Holmes-Tagchungdarpa, Amy. 2014. "Representations of Religion in *The Tibet Mirror*: The Newspaper as Religious Object and Patterns of Continuity and Rupture in Tibetan Material Culture." In *Material Culture and Asian Religions: Text, Image, Object*, edited by Benjamin J. Fleming and Richard D. Mann, 73-93. New York: Routledge.

Imamura, Masao. 2015. "Guest Editorial: Rethinking Frontier and Frontier Studies." *Political Geography* 45: 96-97.

India Arms Act, 1978. Online document. Accessed 15 February 2020. As available at http://www.myanmar-law-library.org/IMG/pdf/the_indian_arms_act.pdf.

Indian Penal Code. Online document. Accessed 10 February 2020. As available at https://www.iitk.ac.in/wc/data/IPC_186045.pdf.

Johnson, Corey, Reece Jones, Anssi Paasi, Louise Amoore, Alison Mountz, Mark Salter, and Chris Rumford. 2011. "Interventions on Rethinking 'the Border' in Border Studies." *Political Geography* 30 (2): 61-69.

Kemenade, Willem, van. 2008. *Détente Between China and India: The Delicate Balance of Geopolitics in Asia.* The Hague: Netherlands Institute of International Relations 'Clingendael'.

Kleemans, Edward R., and Henk G. van de Bunt. 1999. "The social embeddedness of organized crime." *Transnational Organized Crime* 5(2): 19-36.

Kosfeld, Michael. 2005. "Rumours and Markets." *Journal of Mathematical Economics* 41: 646-664. As available at https://ssrn.com/abstract=136728.

Lin, Hsiao-ting. 2006. *Tibet and Nationalist China's Frontier: Intrigues and Ethnopolitics, 1928-49.* Vancouver: UBC Press.

Lodhi, Abdul Q., and Edmund E. Vaz. 1980. "Crime: A Form of Market Transaction." *Canadian Journal of Criminology* 22 (2): 141-150.

Lok Sabha Debates (April 2, 1959). 1959. Parliamentary Debates (Lok Sabha), Vol. XXVIII-No.38: New Delhi.

Ludden, David. 2003. "Presidential Address: Maps in the Mind and the Mobility of Asia." *Journal of Asia Studies* 62 (4): 1057-1078.

Majumdar, Enakshi. 1993. "In Search of a New Resort Emergence of Kalimpong as Hill Station (1865-1920)." *Proceedings of the Indian History Congress* (Indian History Congress) 54: 574-581. Accessed January 01, 2020. https://www.jstor.org/stable/44143030.

Majumdar, Enakshi. 2006. "Emergence of Kalimpong as a Hill Urban Centre." In *Urbanisation in the Eastern Himalayas: Emergence and Issues*, edited by Kurubaki Datta, 173-188. New Delhi: Serials Publications.

Mansfield, Edward D, and Brian Pollins, eds. 2003. *Economic Interdependence and International Conflict: New Perspectives on an Enduring Debate.* Ann Arbor: University of Michigan Press.

Marshall, Jonathan. 1976. "Opium and the Politics of Gangsterism in Nationalist China, 1927-1945." *Bulletin of Concerned Asian Scholars* 8 (3): 19-48. Accessed January 23, 2020. doi:10.1080/14672715.1976.10404414.

Martinez, Oscar J. 1994. *Border People. Life and Society in the U.S.-Mexico Borderlands.* Tucson: University of Arizona Press.

McGranahan, Carole. 2005. "In Rapga's Library: The Texts and Times of a Rebel Tibetan Intellectual." *Cahiers d'Extrême–Asie* 15: 253-274.

McGranahan, Carole. 2017. "Imperial but Not Colonial: Archival Truths, British India, and the Case of the 'Naughty' Tibetans." *Comparative Studies in Society and History* 59 (1): 68-95.

McKay, Alex. 1997. *Tibet and the British Raj : The Frontier Cadre, 1904-1947.* Richmond: Curzon.

McKay, Alex. 2007. *Their Footprints Remain: Biomedical Beginnings Across the Indo-Tibetan Frontier.* Amsterdam: Amsterdam University Press.

McKay, Alex. 2014. "Indifference, Cultural Difference, and a Porous Frontier: Some Remarks on the History of Recreational Drugs in the Tibetan Cultural World." *The Tibet Journal* 39 (1): 53-73.

Mezzadra, Sandro and Brett Neilson. 2013. *Border as Method, or, the Multiplication of Labor.* Durham: Duke University Press.

Mitter, Rana. 2013. *Forgotten Ally: China's World War II, 1937-1945.* Boston, MA: Houghton Mifflin Harcourt.

Moran, Arik, and Warner Catherine. 2016. "Introduction: Charting Himalayan Histories." *Himalaya, the Journal of the Association for Nepal and Himalayan Studies* 35 (2). Accessed January 14, 2020. http://digitalcommons.macalester.edu/himalaya/vol35/iss2/8.

Morrow, James D. 1999. "How Could Trade Affect Conflict?" *Journal of Peace Research* 36: 481-489.

Naylor, Tom R. 2009. "Violence and Illegal Economic Activity: A Deconstruction." *Crime, Law and Social Change* 52 (3): 231-242. Accessed February 19, 2020. doi:DOI 10.1007/s10611-009-9198-9.

Nebesky-Wojkowitz, René, de. 1956. *Where the Gods are Mountains: Three Years Among the People of the Himalayas.* London: Weidenfeld and Nicolson.

Norbu, Dawa. 1997. "Tibet in Sino-Indian Relations: The Centrality of Marginality." *Asia Survey* 37 (11): 1078-1095. Accessed February 23, 2020. https://www.jstor.org/stable/2645742.

Oviedo, Ana Maria, Mark Roland Thomas, and Kamer Karakurum-Özdemir. 2009. *Economic Informality: Causes, Costs, and Policies. A Literature Survey.* World Bank Publication.

Owen, Nicholas. 2003. "The Conservative Party and Indian Independence, 1945-1947." *The Historical Journal* 46 (2): 403-436.

Parker, Bradley J. 2006. "Toward and Understanding of Borderland Processes." *American Antiquity* 71 (1): 77-100.

Pianciola, Niccolò. 2020. "Illegal Markets and the Formation of a Central Asian Borderland: The Turkestan–Xinjiang opium trade (1881–1917)." *Modern Asian Studies.* Accessed March 1, 2020. https://doi.org/10.1017/S0026749X18000227.

Piliavsky, Anastasia. 2013. "Borders without Borderlands: On the Social Reproduction of State Demarcation in Rajastan." In *Borderland Lives in Northern South Asia*, edited by David N. Gellner, 24-46. Durham and London: Duke University Press.

Poddar, Prem, and Lisa Lindkvist Zhang. 2017. "Kalimpong: The China Connection." In *Transcultural Encounters in the Himalayan Borderland: Kalimpong as a "Contact Zone"*, edited by Markus Viehbeck, 149-174. Heidelberg: Heidelberg University Press.

Pratt, Mary Louise. 1991. "Arts of the Contact Zone." *Profession* 91: 33-40.

Provisional Parliamentary Debates. 1950. (1st February to 13th March 1950)." Official Report. First Session of the Parliament of India 1950 (Part I - Questions and Answers), Volume I. Accessed February 18, 2020. https://eparlib.nic.in/bitstream/123456789/760822/1/ppd_08-03-1950.pdf.

Provisional Parliamentary Debates. 1951. (5th February to 31st March 1951)." Parliamentary Debates. Official Report. Third Session of the Parliament of India 1951 (Second Part), Volume VI. Accessed February 18, 2020. https://eparlib.nic.in/bitstream/123456789/760370/1/ppd_10-03-1951.pdf

Ramble, Charles. 1993. "The Name Bhotey." *Himal* 6 (5): 17.

Rawat, Rajiv. 2004. "A Historical Review of Geographic Studies in the Trans-Himalayas." *Trans-Himalayan Studies.* Department of Geography, York University, Toronto, Canada.

Rennie, David Field. 1866. *Bhotan and the Story of the Dooar War.* London: J. Murray.

Reuter, Peter. 1983. *Disorganized Crime: The Economics of the Visible Hand.* Cambridge, MA.: The MIT Press.

Rhodes, Nicholas. 1992. "Tibetan Forgeries Made in Calcutta." *The Numismatic Chronicle* 152: 89-96. Accessed January 21, 2020. https://www.jstor.org/stable/42667835.

Rhodes, Nicholas, Karl Gabrisch, Carlo Valdettaro Pontecorvo della Rocchetta. 1989. *The Coinage of Nepal from the Earliest Times until 1911.* London: Royal Numismatic Society.

Rhodes, Nicholas, and Deki Rhodes. 2006. *A Man of the Frontier: S. W. Laden La (1876-1936): His Life and Times in Darjeeling and Tibet.* Kolkata: Mira Bose.

Rodseth, Lars, and Bradley J. Parker. 2005. "Introduction: Theoretical Considerations in the Study of Frontiers." In *Untaming the Frontiers in Anthropology, Archaeology, and History*, edited by Bradley J. Parker and Lars Rodseth, 3-21. Tucson: University of Arizona Press.

Rumford, Chris. 2012. "Towards a Multiperspectival Study of Borders." *Geopolitics* 17: 887-902.

Sahlins, Peter. 1989. *Boundaries: The Making of France and Spain in the Pyrenees.* Berkeley: University of California Press.

Sangharakshita, Bhikshu. 1991. *Facing Mount Kanchenjunga: An English Buddhist in the Eastern Himalayas.* Glasgow: Windhorse Publications.

Sarkar, Sumit. 1989. *Modern India, 1885-1947.* Basingstoke: Macmillan.

Sawerthal, Anna. 2018. "Babu Tharchin and the 'Tibet Mirror' (Yul phyogs so so'i gsar 'gyur me long, 1925-1963) from Kalimpong." *PhD diss.* Heidelberg : Heidelberg University.

Saxer, Martin, Alessandro Rippa, and Alexander Horstmann. 2018. "Asian Borderlands in a Global Perspective." In *Routledge Handbook of Asian Borderlands*, edited by Alexander Horstmann, Martin Saxer and Alessandro Rippa, 1-14. Abingdon, Oxon.: Routledge.

Schendel, Willem, van. 2005. "Space of Engagement: How Borderlands, Illicit Flows, and Territorial State Interlock." In *Illicit Flows and Criminal Things: States, Borders, and the Other Side of Globalization*, edited by Willem van Schendel and Itty Abraham, 38-68. Bloomington: Indiana University Press.

Schendel, Willem, van, and Itty Abraham. 2005. "Introduction: The Making of Illicitness." In *Illicit Flows and Criminal Things: States, Borders, and the Other Side of Globalization*, edited by Willem van Schendel and Itty Abraham, 1-37. Bloomington: Indian University Press.

Schendel, Willem, van, and Erik de Maaker. 2014. "Asian Borderlands: Introducing their Permeability, Strategic Uses and Meanings." *Journal of Borderland Studies.* Accessed January 14, 2020. doi:10.1080/08865655.2014.892689.

Schneider, Friederick, and Dominik H. Enste. 2000. "Shadow Economies: Size, Causes, and Consequences." *Journal of Economic Literature* 39 (1): 77-114.

Schultz, Kenneth A. 2015. "Borders, Conflict, and Trade." *Annual Review of Political Science* 18, 125-145. DOI: 10.1146/annurev-polisci-020614-095002.

Scott, James C. 2009. *The Art of Not Being Governed: An Anarchist History of Upland Southeast Asia.* New Haven, CT: Yale University Press.

Sen, Tansen. 2021. "The Chinese Intrigue in Kalimpong. Intelligence Gathering and the 'Spies' in a Contact Zone." In *Beyond Pan-Asianism: Connecting China and India, 1840s-1960s*, edited by Tansen Sen and Brian Tsui, 410-459. New Delhi: Oxford University Press.

Shakya, Tsering. 2004. "The Emergence of Modern Tibetan Literature - gsar rtsom." *PhD diss.* London: School of Oriental and African Studies.

Shakya, Tsering. 2013. "The Genesis of the Sino-Tibetan Agreement of 1951." In *The Tibetan History Reader*, edited by Gray Tuttle and Kurtis R. Schaeffer, 609-632. New York; Chichester: Columbia University Press.

Sharma, Jayeeta. 2016. "Producing Himalayan Darjeeling: Mobile People and Mountain Encounters." *Himalaya, the Journal of the Association for Nepal and Himalayan Studies* 35 (2). Accessed January 14, 2020. http://digitalcommons.macalester.edu/himalaya/vol35/iss2/12.

Sherpa, Diki. 2019. "The Transformation of the Indo-Tibetan Trade in Wool, 1904-1962." *China Report* 55 (4): 393-409. doi: 10.1177/0009445519875245.

Simmons, Beth A. 2005. "Rules over Real Estate: Trade, Territorial conflict, and International Borders as Institutions." *Journal of Conflict Resolution* 49: 823-848.

Smith, Warren W. 1996. *Tibetan Nation: A History of Tibetan Nationalism and Sino-Tibetan Relatins.* Boulder, CO: Westview.

Smyer Yü, Dan. 2018. "Introduction: Trans-Himalayas as Multi-state Margins." In *Trans-Himalayan Borderlands: Livelihoods, Territorialities, Modernities*, edited by Dan Smyer Yü and Jean Michaud, 9-32. Amsterdam: Amsterdam University Press.

Smyer Yü , Dan, and Jean Michaud, eds. 2018. *Trans-Himalayan Borderlands: Livelihoods, Territorialities, Modernities.* Amsterdam: Amsterdam University Press.

Soudijn, Melvin R. J. and Edward R. Kleemans. 2009. "Chinese organized crime and situational context: comparing human smuggling and synthetic drugs trafficking." *Crime Law and Social Change* 52: 457-474. DOI 10.1007/s10611-009-9203-3.

Spengen, Wim, van. 2000. *Tibetan Border Worlds: A Geohistorical Analysis of Trade and Traders.* London: Kegal Paul International.

Stoler, Ann Laura. 2002. "Colonial Archives and the Arts of Governance." *Archival Science* 2: 87-109.

Stoler, Ann Laura. 2009. *Along the Archival Grain: Epistemic Anxieties and Colonial Common Sense.* Princeton: Princeton University Press.

Tägil, Sven, Kristian Gerner, Göran Henrikson, Rune Johansson, Ingmar Oldberg, and Kim Salomon. 1977. *Studying Boundary Conflicts: A Theoretical Framework.* Lund, Sweden: Esselte Studium.

Tagliacozzo, Eric. 2005. *Secret Trades, Porous Borders: Smuggling and States Along a Southeast Asian Frontier, 1865-1915.* New Haven, CT: Yale University Press.

Tagliacozzo, Eric. 2009. "Contraband and Violence: Lessons from the Southeast Asian Case." *Crime, Law and Social Change* 52: 243-252.

Talbot, Ian. 1998. *Pakistan: A Modern History.* London: Hurst & Co.

Talbot, Ian, and Gurharpal Singh. 1999. *Region and Partition: Bengal, Punjab and the Partition of the Subcontinent.* Oxford: Oxford University Press.

Tendler, Judith. 2002. "Small Firms, the Informal Sector, and the Devil's Deal." *IDS Bulletin* 33 (3): 1-15. https://doi.org/10.1111/j.1759-5436.2002.tb00035.x.

Thai, Philip. 2018. *China's War on Smuggling. Law, Economic Life, and the Making of the Modern State, 1842-1965.* New York: Columbia University Press.

Titeca, Kristof, and Rachel Flynn. 2010. "Regulation, Cross-Border Trade and Practical Norms in West Nile, North-Western Uganda." *Africa* 80 (4): 573-594.

Vasantkumar, Chris. 2017. "Odd Neighbours: Trans-Himalayan Tibetan Itineraries and Chinese Economic Development." In *The Art of Neighbouring: Making Relations Across China's Borders*, edited by Martin Saxer and Juan Zhang, 167-186. Amsterdam: Amsterdam University Press.

Vasquez, John A. 2009. *The War Puzzle Revisited.* Cambridge: Cambridge University Press.

Vasquez, John A. and Marie T. Henehan. 2001. "Territorial Disputes and the Probability of War, 1816–1992." *Journal of Peace Research* 38: 123-138.

Viehbeck, Markus. 2017. "Introduction: Cultural History as a History of Encounters - A 'Contact Perspective'." In *Transcultural Encounters in the Himalayan Borderlands: Kalimpong as a "Contact Zone"*, edited by Markus Viehbeck, 1-22. Heidelberg: Heidelberg University Press.

Walsh, Ernest Herbert. 1973. *The coinage of Nepal.* Delhi: Indological Book House.

Weatherley, Robert. 2006. *Politics in China Since 1949: Legitimazing Authoritarian Rule.* Abingdon, Oxon; New York: Routledge.

Webb, Justin W., Laszlo Tihanyi, R. Duane Ireland, and David G. Sirmon. 2009. "You Say Illegal, I Say Legitimate: Entrepreneurship in the Informal Economy." *The Academy of Management Review* 34 (3): 492-510. Accessed January 18, 2020. https://www.jstor.org/stable/27760016.

Webster, Donovan. 2003. *The Burma Road: The Epic Story of the China-Burma-India Theater in World War II.* New York: Farrar, Straus and Giroux.

Wendl, Tobias, and Michael Rösler. 1999. "Introduction: Frontier and Borderlands. The Rise and Relevance of an Anthropological Research Genre." In *Frontiers and Borderlands: Anthropological Perspectives*, edited by Michael Rösler and Tobias Wendl, 1-27. Frankfurt am Main: Peter Lang.

Whitaker, Reg. 2002. "The Dark Side of Life: Globalisation and International Crime." *Socialist Register* 38 (A World of Contradictions), edited by Leo Panitch and Colin Leys: 131-151. Accessed February 03, 2020. https://socialistregister.com/index.php/srv/article/view/5780.

Wilkinson, Glenn R. 1995. "At the Coal-Face of History: Personal Reflections on Using Newspapers as a Source." *Studies in Newspapers and Periodical History* 3 (1-2): 211-221. Accessed January 16, 2020. doi:10.1080/13688809509357927.

Wimmer, Andreas, and Brian Min. 2006. "From Empire to Nation-State: Explaining Wars in the Modern World, 1816-2001." *American Sociological Review* 71 (6): 867-897. Accessed January 11, 2020.

Witte, Ann Dryden, Kelly Eakin, and Carl P. Simon. 1982. *Beating the System: The Underground Economy.* Boston, Mass.: Praeger.

Wong, Diana. 2005. "The Rumor of Trafficking: Border Controls, Illegal Migration, and the Sovereignty of the Nation-State." In *Illicit Flows and Criminal Things: States, Borders, and the Other Side of Globalization*, edited by Willem van Schendel and Itty Abraham, 69-100. Bloomington: Indian University Press.

World Economic Report 1948. Department of Economic Affairs of the United Nations. 1949. *World Economic Report 1948.* World economic report, New York: United Nations Publications. Accessed February 12, 2020. https://www.un.org/en/development/desa/policy/wess/wess_archive/searchable_archive/1948_WESS_Full.pdf.

Wright, Richard N.J. 1992. "The Debasement of the Republican Silver Coinage of Yunnan Province." *The Numismatic Chronicle* 152: 97-109. Accessed February 13, 2020. https://www.jstor.org/stable/42667836.

Zhang, Huasha. 2021. "The Sedan Chair vs the Steamboat: The Sichuan Route and the Maritime Route in the Making of Modern Sino-Tibetan Relations." *Modern Asian Studies*: 1-40. DOI:10.1017/S0026749X20000220